Advanced Mediumship

A Masterful Guide
for the Practicing Medium

Mary-Anne Kennedy

Published by:
Library Tales Publishing
www.LibraryTalesPublishing.com
www.Facebook.com/LibraryTalesPublishing

Published in New York, New York.

For general information on our other products and services, please contact our Customer Care Department at 1-800-754-5016, or fax 917-463-0892. For technical support, please visit
www.LibraryTalesPublishing.com

Library Tales Publishing also publishes its books in a variety of electronic formats. Every content that appears in print is available in electronic books.

978-1-956769-51-7
978-1-956769-52-4

Table of Contents

For all the students who have trusted me to teach them on their mediumship journey.

For the great many people who have chosen me to connect them to their loved ones in spirit.

For the spirit world and its infinite wisdom and love.

For my dad in spirit, Wayne, who continues to be a great gift in my life.

And for Ryan, August, and Culzean; forever in my corner, as I am in yours.

Thank you. I love you.

Foreword

Our lives intersected with Mary-Anne's following tragedy. This may come as no surprise to you, the reader, as many who have experienced the loss of a loved one often start to look deeper into their spiritual beliefs. Mary-Anne has given evidentiary medium readings to so many who have experienced personal tragedy and loss throughout her years of practice.

In our circumstance, our energetic and healthy son, Zach and his beautiful partner, Kaya, both only 21, passed suddenly in a tragic kayak accident in 2016. As many who have lost loved ones, we wondered if their vibrant lives ended when they passed or if it was possible that consciousness and personality existed in a spiritual form. We were fortunate to have a close friend connect us with having a mediumship reading quite soon after Zach and Kaya passed. Although, as health professionals trained in the scientific method, we admittedly approached the reading with a lot of skepticism. The medium, however, brought through such personal and verifiable messages that only our family and Zach could know that it left us with a new hopeful possibility that Zach and Kaya may in fact still be present in our lives, albeit in spiritual form. This started us on a new path moving forward.

We believe the profound grief experienced by the loss of a loved one is one of the worst adversities that a person will experience in their lives. Unfortunately, as a family we are not strangers to extreme loss as we have been living within the confines of extreme physical disability for 15 years. Jeff was diagnosed with the debilitating and incurable neurological disease amyotrophic lateral sclerosis (ALS) in 2007 when he was only 41. With all the personal losses that we have gone through, the physical losses of Zach and Kaya will be forever the most painful and challenging of our adversities. In our experience, opening to the spiritual life of our passed loved ones has made our grief more manageable and lighter.

Mary-Anne synchronistically entered our lives early in our spiritual journey. Darlene decided that she needed more validation and while searching out a medium, she purchased a ticket for herself and Kaya's mom to attend an introduction to mediumship afternoon workshop taught by Mary-Anne. Following this Darlene arranged a private reading. Mary-Anne delivered messages from Zach with astonishing accuracy, kindness and compassion. To our amazement there were also specific messages provided during the reading that we would only be able to verify months later! These validations provided immense comfort and solidified our new belief that Zach and Kaya were undeniably still spiritually alive and present in our lives! Later that year, Darlene gifted Jeff and Zach's brothers, '6 weeks of Messages from Spirit' with Mary-Anne. These were full of love, support and advice from Zach and contained lots of evidence that it was Zach talking with us. Some of the wisdoms Mary-Anne brought through from Zach are in Jeff's best-selling memoir, Still Life. Mary- Anne has greatly helped us deepen our connection with Zach, both directly and indirectly. We now know that love transcends the boundary between the physical and the spiritual.

Recognizing how difficult it was to get ourselves on a healing path from the depths of our grief and acknowledging this is a lifelong journey, both our family and Kaya's family, founded the Zach Sutherland and Kaya Firth Resiliency Foundation and established a website called choose2beresilient.com. This registered charity, named in honour of Kaya and Zach, provides post-secondary scholarships in recognition of youth who are resilient following the loss of their loved one(s).

Acknowledging the importance that a spiritual connection has made to our healing journey, we also decided that as an offering to our community, we would host 'An Evening with Spirit'. These evenings are particularly helpful for those individuals who are curious or uncertain and would like to broaden their understanding of mediumship and spirituality. We were beyond grateful when Mary-Anne generously offered her services as the evidential medium for the event. These evenings were enthusiastically received and were always sold out. Mary-Anne delivered evidential messages from Spirit to a considerable number of grateful attendees. We were mesmerized by Mary-Anne's talent in this environment. It would be difficult to leave this event with any skepticism. This event has become one of our most sought out fundraisers for Zach and Kaya's Resiliency Foundation.

We have talked about some of the direct ways that Mary-Anne has helped us form a connection to the spiritual. These speak to Mary-Anne's incredible talent as an evidentiary medium. Although these abilities are amazing, perhaps her greatest gift is as a teacher of evidentiary mediumship. We have witnessed since Kaya and Zach's passing, the development of fantastic medium skills under Mary-Anne's guidance in three of our very close friends. Mary-Anne has taught them the importance of providing the sitter with evidential messages from their loved one that are verifiable and resonate. Most importantly, she has mentored her students to deliver messages from Spirit with the compassion, kindness and love intended by Spirit. In our minds, sharing her processes of evidentiary mediumship is Mary-Anne's greatest talent! We believe you will come to realize this yourself as you read and practice the skills so beautifully shared by Mary-Anne in her second book, Advanced Mediumship: A Masterful Guide for the Practicing Medium.

- Jeff and Darlene Sutherland

Introduction

Talking to the other side is probably one of the least conventional occupations that exists. But if you are reading this, then you have no-doubt made peace with your out-of-the-ordinary role of 'conduit-between-worlds'. If you have not yet found your comfort zone in this work, this book aims to bring you there.

You might feel pulled in different directions as you search for greater fulfillment in your life. So let me start by saying this to you: Bravo. Well done, you brave soul! You have embraced a level of courage, truly, that most people dare not dream of. You have listened to the call of your soul, which has asked you to pay attention to the subtleties in this universe, and to become a bridge for love and healing between this world and the next.

Along your journey so far, you may have found that a good many mediumship students – even those who demonstrate a tremendous ability to evidentially channel spirit people – halt their own progression because they fear being wrong or failing. You have probably visited this mental space yourself, a time or two. All mediums have faced that fear at some point; but not everyone pushes past it. If you have pushed past it already or, you are working on it now (more on that later), then you are well on your way to a successful professional practice.

You are exactly where you are supposed to be, and you are going where you are meant to go. If you are not sure that you are ready for this next step in your mediumship, I offer this to you: We are never off-course. Every experience, whether perceived positively or negatively, holds a treasure – a lesson or opportunity for growth — that our souls have asked to experience. So carry forward in your pursuit of advanced and professional mediumship with the knowledge that it will bring you all that you need.

I cannot tell you how many students I have trained in mediumship and mentored throughout their spiritual journey. There have been so many. But all of them were able to learn to communicate with spirit. Yes, all of them, without exception. And of those who were trained, a large number of them have gone into their own professional mediumship practices. So with this reality in mind - that there are lots of spiritual schools and teachers turning out more and more trained mediums every year - you might ask - How can I set myself apart from everyone else doing the same thing I am doing? It is a valid question, and mediumship aside, one that should be asked before you pursue any career. From a business perspective, it is often helpful to differentiate yourself from others and this can be done in a number of ways. It will pay off to give some attention to this part of defining your spiritually-centered business model, and I will talk more about this throughout the book. But all of the above is only significant if you have absorbed and incorporated the fundamental components needed in a successful mediumship practice, which requires far more energy and focus than just business planning. If you truly want to tap into your purpose as a medium and make a mark on the people who come to see you, what you must absorb and incorporate is a deep understanding of your role, your responsibility, and how to deliver the miracle that is spirit communication.

The power of mediumship is only partly found in a person's ability to receive and deliver on-point, validating information that demonstrates continuity of the soul beyond physical death. The truer measure of the power and purpose of mediumship lies in its ability to create a shift within another. To clarify, a shift is what brings someone closer to a state of wellness and healing, closer to oneness and unity, and closer to themselves – even if these are gradual processes and do not occur instantaneously. More succinctly, the gauge of good, purposeful mediumship is not and cannot rely only on the medium's raw ability to channel spirit. The majority of the gauge must be placed in the receiver. The subject and center of the story of any mediumship reading, from a medium's perspective, must be the other. And while this does not mean it is our responsibility as mediums to make shifts happen in people's lives, we do want to deliver our work in ways that allow for its full potential to be realized. Our goal must be to give the people who come to see us the greatest chance at experiencing a positive change in their lives. If you cause any level of shift to occur and it is moving in a forward direction – toward healing and understanding — then you can count that as a positive contribution to life, and the mark of meaningful work. And that is the reason for writing this book - to teach you how to shift from being simply a medium, to being a great one, more than just a raw channel - MORE than a medium.

Meaningful contributions to life are where purpose comes in, but purpose itself is not defined by the role you assume. In other words, no one's purpose in life is to be a medium. Purpose is about what meaningful soul qualities we bring into expression, or bring into the form reality in some way. So if part of your soul's purpose (what you, at a soul-level planned to do, express, and experience in this incarnation) is to bring the qualities of understanding and forgiveness into the world of form, then being a medium might be a great role to assume because it lends itself to the frequent and powerful expression of those qualities. When we choose to work as a medium and to put our deepest wishes to heal another into this work, we are truly living a life with purpose.

No matter what specific form it takes, purpose will always relate to making positive contributions to some form of life on earth. So whether your purpose is expressed through the form of being a medium, a school teacher, a therapist, or a manager, it really does not matter, so long as your purpose aligns with an action or role that allows for the expression of that purpose. If your contributions to life relate to expressing qualities such as unconditional love, grace, and compassion, then truly you can find purpose in anything you do, whether or not you are assuming a particular role. So, finding that soul purpose (which again is not a role or job you fulfill but rather qualities you are here to express and share with others), is an imperative on the soul journey. Identifying it will add a level of meaning and allow you to create conscious alignment that you could not imagine without actually discovering it.

If you are authentically drawn to the spirit world and helping others to heal, it is likely your soul purpose (the qualities you are here to bring into form) will include the expression of unconditional love, compassion, understanding, joy, presence, and learning, just to name a few.

If the basics of mediumship are new to you, be sure to precede reading this book with my first book, *How to Become a Medium: A Step-by-Step Guide to Connecting with the Other Side*. In this, my second book on the subject of mediumship, my intention in writing it is that it will be of assistance to you as you expand not only your abilities as a medium, but as you expand your own consciousness, thereby increasing your capacity to be of service in this world. I am happy you are here and that we can take this journey together.

~ Mary-Anne

Chapter One

Welcome to the World of Spirit
A Deeper Level

§

People often wonder what it is like to see a spirit person – you must have been asked this question once or twice in your mediumship journey. Most folks are terribly surprised to learn that spirit people, in fact, do not look like anything. They no longer have a form body, but rather are made of an energy body. It is the essence or soul of the person that remains alive and well – this is what essence without form is – it is pure spirit.

For those who are clairvoyant, they do in fact 'see' spirit – a face, a body, a distinguishing feature. But when we see this, we are subconsciously translating their energy through our own minds to determine what they looked like. Other times we are receptive to the telepathic projection of an image which is best explained as an image of what the spirit person looked like when they were here. Sometimes, it is a spitting image of how they looked at some point in their life. At other times, their appearance is just a representative likeness. And while spirit can, in fact, manipulate energy within the universe to manifest as a form for very brief periods of time as an apparition, their essential state exists only in formlessness. They do not 'look' like anything. I have worked with many excellent student mediums who never really thought of spirit 'not looking like anything' because most of their experiences were clairvoyantly-based, and spirit did, in fact, look like something. But of course, you know that their physical bodies have departed existence and are no longer animated. That body their soul previously occupied has no physical substance left. When you see them in their earthly bodies, most commonly, it is a mental image transfer of what they did look like in life so that their person here in the physical world might recognize them. Still, I have trained many mediums who never once saw what a spirit person looked like. It was not part of how they perceived or received information, and so offering a physical description of the spirit person was not possible, nor was it needed, since physical description is but one piece of information.

There is a common misconception among non-mediums that spirits speak to us, directly using a voice. In fact, just as spirits no longer have physical bodies and therefore no longer look like anything, it is also true that they do not have voice boxes and cannot 'speak' to us. Now, this does not mean we do not perceive information through what sounds like a voice speaking, because some mediums do hear information from spirit. And while spirit will sometimes use various universally-present energies to transmit sound, including a voice, what is usually occurring when mediums hear voices is a mental 'cloaking' as I like to call it, of vibrational information so that it makes conscious sense to us in some way.

Vibrational information (non-form information communicated from spirit) perceived by you will be 'cloaked' in your own mind, and this cloaking happens not through conscious choice but instead, subconsciously. For example, if a spirit person wants to communicate with you they took very good care of their appearance, had their hair done regularly, wore makeup, and selected their clothing carefully, your mind may subconsciously translate that vibrational information by bringing it in to your conscious awareness as a mental image of a dolled-up woman, or hearing the words "took care of self" in your own mind. Or, it might be simpler, or more subtle in that you might know or feel that this person took care of their personal appearance. This is partly why mediumship can be so difficult to master. Most of the communication is non-linear and symbolic. As mediums, we must learn to interpret the meaning of what spirit is communicating. Further, we must accept and allow our imaginations to be in a state of play. We cannot constrain the mind by expecting things to come to us in specific ways. We must allow the cloaking, however bizarre it might seem, and allow for changes in symbolic meaning over time. This is a great approach for the evolving, growing medium.

When I think about the power of spirit – about who they are and how they relate to us here in the physical world, I think about their ever-present support and guidance. They reveal a great willingness to help us by relaying insightful, compassionate, and loving messages. Spirit does so much behind the scenes that we do not know about. They are master orchestrators, weaving synchronistic events into our lives each and every day. So often, a client has said to me, "when I booked this session for a reading and was given today's date, I knew it was meant to be because today is the anniversary of their passing." This is but one example of how spirit plays in our lives, assisting, guiding, and comforting us. But still, and without fail, I am equally in awe of the power of the living human spirit that, as mediums, we bear witness to all the time.

As mediums, we have the privilege of witnessing the power of the living human spirit as it reveals itself through the people left behind after loss. The courage of these grief-bearers can be seen in how they find a way to keep on going. Their bravery is highlighted by their willingness to speak the names of the ones they have lost. And their strength is demonstrated by the purpose they regain after surviving something their loved one did not. These people – the ones who picked up the shattered pieces of themselves, pulled out the devastating shards of glass from the deepest wounds, and continued to walk through the fire of afterloss to reach some space of being able to live their lives again – these are the people whose lives mirror the strength and beauty of spirit. They embody what it means to be resilient, hopeful, compassionate and to be loving toward oneself. And somewhere along the way, they are leaving gifts for those who have yet to find their way through the darkness. This inner power to carry on, even amidst chaos and ash, is indeed a manifestation of universal strength and the power of spirit imbuing itself into us here in the physical.

I have been asked a number of times in interviews and conversations what I find to be most rewarding in my work as a medium. I have many responses but the one that always comes to mind first is helping someone come full-circle in their journey through grief. It is incredibly fulfilling to accompany someone on their journey through an initial mediumship reading, into becoming a student of mediumship, into becoming a professional with their own practice. How wonderful is it to approach this work from a place of deep, personal, lived experience? And how empowering is it to take some of the darkest experiences of our lives in loss, and turn them into service, to help others who are experiencing the same? Yes, this is empowered, heart-based, conscious living, in all its glory. I have found so often that the most compassionate (and often the most talented) mediums I have trained, have their own lived experiences of grief and loss. This is another glimmer of the light that can be created out of a deep wound. It is the form-world manifestation of the universal truth that light is available after the dark.

All along the journey of loss, spirit is everywhere, supporting the survivors with patience and love. Spirit desires their recovery; not back into the person they once were, because that can never be. But into the new version of themselves – the one that has walked around with a gaping hole in their being, while also growing new skin, and slowly re-birthing themselves. The re-birth often happens around the loss, because that is where the new tissue grows. The growth comes from the wound, like a shoot from a seed buried in the dirt. And as advanced or professional mediums, it is part of our role to support this healing and new growth, providing comfort, wisdom, and sometimes direction to those who are suffering. If you came to this work from loss as I did, then you understand how pivotal it was to feel embraced by a supportive voice around you – someone who could help you navigate through the muddy waters.

Not everyone can see the power of spirit being animated and emerging out of the lives of those left behind, but as a medium, you most certainly have, even if you have not yet recognized this beautiful reality just yet. I often think about all of the people I have worked with who radically transformed after loss – from becoming mediums, to healers, to starting support groups, writing books, sponsoring awards, and events…the list is endless. Each and every one of those acts, in the name of a loved one, is the face of spirit. Their legacy can be found in the indelible marks they left behind and which animate the actions of those still here – always for the good. How amazing is that?

I remember a number of years ago meeting two families who had lost their young-adult children unexpectedly and devastatingly on a sunny winter day. Their grief was crippling and overwhelming. I could imagine their darkest days and what must have been reeling through their minds and ripping through their hearts. Somehow, over time, they mustered up the energy and courage to continue on - to keep living.

One of the ways they came to continue the legacy of their children was through a scholarship fund. The scholarships are awarded to people who themselves have suffered debilitating loss in their lives, and it offers them help to forge ahead in academic studies. I have always seen this as a powerful and positive ripple effect from a dark and devastating sinkhole in the deepest ocean. And I think as mediums, we have to notice the ripple effect - we have to be able to speak to those we are in service to, and help them understand that recovery from loss is possible. We have to know this, either through our own lived experiences, or through the experiences of others we bear witness to. It is so important to be able to see, to notice, first hand, that recovery is possible.

While the creation of the scholarship fund was an important effort to contribute to the world, there was yet another brilliant gift that surfaced after the losses. While each family began some degree of spiritual study and exploration, one of the mothers in fact began the study and practice of mediumship development. No doubt, she did this out of a deep desire to connect with her child, but also to experience the beauty of the spirit world. Incredibly, of all the mediums I have taught and trained directly out of loss to this day, she was and is, the most rawly-talented, with exceptional skill and mediumship abilities. There it is…another spark of light. The ripple effect. I often think of all the people and families who have been helped in this world because of their courage and desire to honour their loved ones in spirit. For these the two families, it might be a small consolation for their loss, but to the rest of the world, their efforts in paying tribute to their loved ones in spirit have made a positive impact, exponentially.

Chapter Two

More than a Medium

§

Mediumship in and of itself is the demonstration, through evidence, of the continuity of soul and the preservation of consciousness (essence) after physical death. And thus the primary role of the medium is to be an open and clear conduit to receive information from spirit, to understand it, and then to communicate it to someone in the living. Developing the ability to serve as a clear channel, to interpret, and to relay, is paramount in becoming the best medium you can be. But what you will soon learn is that once you reach that state of consistent accuracy, consistent connection, and consistent power in your readings, spirit and human life will begin to pull you into a whole new level of service.

As your experience broadens and deepens, you will find there will be readings where your raw ability to be a medium is just not enough. It is not enough to take your sitter from a state of grief to a single moment of lightness. You could bring through the most compellingly accurate information, and yet, your sitter remains unmoved. It will be these readings in which you will expand your role beyond just your connection with spirit to include serving as your sitters' grief counsellor, life coach, and deep listener. It will be these readings that show you there is so much more to being a powerful medium than just being a good conduit for the spirit world.

As you develop, however, it will be important to stay clear about what your job is. As a medium, people generally come to sit with you to witness continuity of the soul. So at the most basic level, that is what you will endeavour to do. And you must know, so long as you have done so, to the best of your ability, that you have fulfilled your sacred agreement of communication with the spirit world. Whether or not the transmission of spirit's information proved to be transformative to someone here in the physical world is not really our concern as mediums. Sure we want to make an impact, we want to help. But our primary role, truly, is to represent spirit and transmit information. Our role is not to ensure a healing experience (although we often do). Many times in readings, people are not ready or able to hear and process information that comes through. For example, I can recall reading for a woman whose father had recently passed. There were a number of misdeeds that had occurred in their relationship (on both sides), and when her father came through to speak about some of them and to apologize, she was not yet ready to accept it. She was still angry and unsettled inside. When her father in spirit made the apology, it was met by a raising of the eyebrows and a defensive facial expression. And I had to be okay with that. Six months or a year later, she might have been able to consider his new perspective from the spirit world and stepped in to forgiveness (for him and herself), but at that moment, it simply fell short and carried very little meaning for her. If I had been unclear about my essential role as a medium and felt it was also my responsibility to somehow bring healing to her journey, I would have been very disappointed in myself and my inability to provide that to her. But instead, I understood that my job is to relay information, and if and when someone here is ready to receive it for all it is worth, they will. Ultimately, timing is not up to me and it is not up to you. I am ok with that and you should be too.

When we want to be our best at something and take fulfillment from it, we must always make sure we are growing and learning. There is no 'arrival point' in mediumship. You can achieve any accomplishment in the world, and that accomplishment, in the context of your entire life, will be just one thing, one day, one moment in time - like a drop in the bucket. And even if the achievement is long worked-for, once achieved, you will for certain go looking for opportunities for growth and change and learning afterward. The journey in mediumship is never over, and in fact, the journey really is the point of it all. There really and truly is no destination. Keeping that in mind, setting a goal for yourself and striving for it is important. Just remember that we really only feel fulfilled when we keep learning, not just when we succeed in achieving something.

I remember so many instances where I was sure I would feel fulfilled on the mediumship journey after achieving a goal – whether it was publishing a book, selling out an event, starting a school, winning awards or getting a television show. In fact, just becoming a professional medium. But once achieved, those successes were just things (very rewarding, to be sure), but I never arrived anywhere where I said, "okay, I have done it all now and I feel totally fulfilled". Rather, I just kept pushing with the thirst to know more, to be more for myself and my clients and the people closest to me, to expand my own consciousness, to be more loving, and to continue to experience adventure and wonder in my life. If there is one thing I know from spirit after performing thousands of readings and spending countless hours in communication is that life is for living, and the more we live and the more we love, the better a life truly is.

When it comes to continuing to challenge yourself and growing as a medium (and as a result, getting continuously better at mediumship), it is often helpful to periodically examine how your readings are going and gauge if any improvements can be made. From a fundamental viewpoint, mediumship can be broken down into three micro- steps or processes.

The first of these processes is INPUT.

> Input is receiving information from spirit. As mediums, we prepare ourselves energetically to become clear and present, and raise our vibrational state through conscious intention and meditation. Raising our vibration or the quality of our essence (the quality of our energy), we become a close vibrational match to spirit, and when we do this, spirit is able to enter in to our energy and blend with us. Once we have blended or merged with spirit, we are able to discern information from them - we are able to receive them. It is interesting to note that

over the years, in the training of hundreds of mediums, that many of them have believed prior to working with me that during mediumship, spirit people are communicating at a distance; that is, transmitting information to the receiver from outside of the receiver, itself. While spirit can in fact communicate this way, in true, genuine mediumship, we are blended or merged with the spirit person. It is like we are dancing with them - our energies intertwined. Most of the time in mediumship, the reality is that the information you receive, present, and validate feels like it is coming from inside of you rather than 'out there somewhere'.

The second aspect of the mediumship process is INTERNAL CONSCIOUS OR SUBCONSCIOUS TRANSLATION.

The language of spirit is mostly symbolic, and sometimes literal. For example, a spirit person may show you an image of a coin, which you may interpret as them being a coin collector. The coin, to you, either consciously or subconsciously means coin collector. Upon presenting this information to your sitter, you learn the spirit person did not collect coins but had given the sitter a special coin when they were a child. Often, we are aware of whether or not a piece of information is representing something symbolically or is to be taken literally, and other times we simply do not know. Further, there are times when our translation was never meant to occur and spirit intended us to receive that information completely literally. Throughout a reading, you will be switching constantly between literal and symbolic communication from the other side. The internal translation is making sense of the symbolic information, and even the literal information requires that you place it in context. The translation is what allows us to understand what spirit people are communicating to us. When we translate consciously, we identify a symbol and assign a meaning to it, either in the exact moment the symbol is presented to us, or, as in the case of a familiar symbol that you have successfully interpreted many times before, you quickly assign a previously determined meaning to it. When we subconsciously translate information from spirit, we are, what I call, 'cloaking' non-form information so that we may understand it in literal terms. I began calling this act 'cloaking' in my teaching because it reminded me of a cartoon I used to watch when I was a kid. In the cartoon, there was a ghost in the house and the ghost could see everyone and everything going on around it, but no one could see the ghost. The people in the house had a sense that something was present, but they could not discern anything beyond a feeling. That was until someone decided to throw a sheet over the area they had a feeling in to see if there was anything there. Lo and behold, the ghost took form and everyone could see it! The sheet being cloaked over the non-form-being made it discernible to the eye, visible in some way that we, here in the physical plane, could understand.

And so in mediumship, when we receive vibrational information from spirit, we must allow our minds to 'throw a sheet over it', or, cloak it. By allowing the information to be cloaked by the mind, you surrender to the mind totally and trust that it will do what it needs to do. The cloaking has to be subconscious rather than directed by us. Our subconscious minds work very well as practicing mediums, so allow your subconscious the freedom to do its work. In order for us to make sense of non-form information, our minds must wrap it up in ways that we can understand. And that may mean when a grandmother energy-in-spirit comes near to you, you recall your own grandmother. Or you may smell the scent of her old perfume. Or you may see an image of an older woman. We all cloak in different ways. How my subconscious mind cloaks will be different from yours, so it is important to avoid comparing how others consciously interpret or make sense subconsciously of the language of spirit.

What does all of this about cloaking mean, and why is it important? It means you do not need to take everything literally!

In fact, when you step out of thinking that everything communicated to you is to be taken literally, your mediumship will get radically better. Get comfortable in the subtle, get comfortable in the world of symbolic meaning where an image, a feeling, a memory of your own needs to be translated and related to spirit or your sitter.

The ways in which you receive or translate information may be different from how other mediums receive and translate – even if it is through the same clairsense (clairvoyance - seeing, claircognizance - knowing, clairaudience - hearing, clairsentience - feeling). Be okay with that! You must accept and allow your imagination to be at play in mediumship. Do not constrain your mind by expecting things to come to you in certain ways. Allow the cloaking, however bizarre.

The third micro-step in mediumship is OUTPUT. Output is relaying the information from spirit to your sitter. Doing this part well includes delivering with compassion, recognizing truth without distortion, and communicating clearly and confidently.

Journal Exercise: Input, Translation, Output

> Ask yourself, "Which part of my mediumship (input, translation, output) is the most challenging for me right now? What could use some extra focus or fine-tuning?"

Depending on your answer, here are some guidelines for improving one of the micro-steps that make up the entire process of mediumship. Keep in mind that it is helpful to work on one aspect at a time, tending to the most important, first. For example, it makes more sense to start working on the quality of your blend or merge with spirit to get better at input before focusing on upping your translation or output. Why? If you can not blend well with spirit, your translating and delivery will be the least of your concerns!

Improving INPUT

Improving input means examining your preparation time, including setting your intentions, clearing yourself and your space, opening your chakras, and reaching inner stillness and presence, thereby raising your vibration.

Are you doing all of these things? This examination also means asking yourself, "what is my consciousness (my essence or essential nature) during a reading and in my ordinary life? Is there a big disparity between the two?" Further ask yourself, "Am I able to identify with and relay messages of understanding, forgiveness, tolerance, etc. from spirit without distortion if, I, myself, am frequently experiencing expressions of judgment, of anger, of blame?"

This self-examination is intended to highlight the shadows in our own consciousness so that we may recognize and embrace them. And once we do so, we can then invite the positive-opposite qualities into our consciousness that once expressed frequently will, in turn, obliterate the shadows. Examples of this include shifting from blame to forgiveness, or from worry to trust, or from fear to courage. As we evolve and grow our own consciousness, we become more spirit-like, and are much less likely to distort the messages from the other side – as can happen when we want to give others what they want to hear, or when we want to make ourselves look good or simply, because we do not know any better.

Take another moment to ask yourself, "Is there something in my consciousness that has the potential to affect my merge/blend with spirit?" Or perhaps, it would be better phrased for some as, "In what ways am I least spirit-like?" Are there parts of your current personality that put you out of alignment with spirit? Consider all these things when working on the INPUT of mediumship, the front-end part of the process.

Thoughts to consider: We must become more spirit-like in order to deliver clear, undistorted messages from the other side.

Improving PROCESSING/TRANSLATION

Learning to interpret the symbolic nature of spirit communication takes a lot of time, so do not feel rushed! You know spirit will use your own terms of reference as much as possible by having you recall things you have done, people you know, experiences you have had in life because they want you to speak about the same idea as it relates to them and their life, or the life of the person for whom you are reading.

The more readings you do, the easier it becomes to understand symbols because you will start to experience recurring symbols, solidifying their meanings. How do we know if something is literal or symbolic? For example, is an image of an apple, without context, symbolic of a teacher? Or, could it literally be referencing an apple because the sitter went apple picking yesterday? It is true that the more experience you have, the clearer your understanding of the image will be but, even in professional work, there will certainly be moments where you are still not sure. And so you must explore it both ways with your sitter – symbolically and literally. It is ok to do that a few times in a reading. For example, if we go back to the apple as a potential symbol versus a literal communication, I might say to my client if I am unsure whether or not to interpret the apple literally or symbolically, "I am being shown an apple, so they are either trying to acknowledge a teacher or you have done something with apples in the last couple of days. Can you understand this?"

As you continue to explore information both symbolically and literally, you will become more fluent in your understanding as to whether a communication requires translation at all, and if so, your library of meaning will be so robust that you are naturally confident making sense of anything transmitted to you from spirit.

Improving OUTPUT

Of course, each of us has our own personality, and we express ourselves accordingly. In mediumship however, it is so important to contain our own personalities if they are going to trump the nature of the spirit we are representing. What is meant by this? Let us assume that you have now come into your own style of mediumship delivery. For example, you might have found that part of your style is to bring humour into your readings straight away. Now imagine that you are in communication with a spirit who, in fact, had little to no humour in their personality at all. Do not let your chosen presentation style lead the way here; you must honour and represent the spirit person true to their nature. You are their voice, so allow it to be so without distorting their voice with your own. This is what it means to truly honour spirit by never allowing your own personality to supersede the nature of the spirit person you are representing.

Another opportunity to improve output comes through enacting what I call the Heart Filter, which is a set of spiritual principles that help to guide our work as mediums. As information comes to you and you process and interpret it, it must pass through the Heart Filter before the information is delivered outward. The Heart Filter is essentially asking these questions: Is this truth? Is this kind? Is this necessary/useful? If we can answer "Yes" to all of these questions, then we may proceed in passing along the information we are receiving. Now these questions may sound easy to answer, but sometimes it can be easy to miss that a piece of information, or the language in which we choose to express it, is actually contravening one of these spiritual principles.

Consider the following example. During a reading you become aware of a very traumatic passing in great detail. You understand the necessity of establishing cause of passing in your reading, and your personality is such that you call it as you see it. You are blunt, and you know it. You now have a choice: be allegiant to your personality and describe it exactly as you see it without sparing any details. Or, choose to be consistent with spirit and heart-based service, and describe the passing truthfully while omitting any unnecessary graphic details in order to still be truthful and validating. Now this might lead you to ask the question: "Aren't we supposed to give everything we get?"

Well, generally the answer to this question is yes. But is this an absolute? It is not. It is not an absolute. The most important guiding principle in mediumship is to help people; here and on the other side. Here is another example: a spirit person wants to apologize for misdeeds they committed against your client/sitter. In that communication, you learn from spirit what the misdeeds were. They were extensively abusive toward your client, and naming those offenses out loud could make your sitter feel overly exposed and vulnerable. Is it okay to relay these offenses you learned from spirit graphically? Since spirit communicated them to you, does this mean you must name the acts? The answer is no. You must not re-traumatize someone. You may communicate the apology for misdeeds without specifying them so that the message is passed along, but no further harm should take place.

Taking into consideration all of the aspects of output and making any necessary adjustments as needed will no-doubt improve the quality of your mediumship work.

Chapter Three

The Empath, the Psychic, and the Medium

§

Being empathic is such a gift! Identifying with another so deeply is a service to this world because it obliterates the notion that we are all separate from each other. The empath experiences the world as ultra-connected. As empaths, of course, we must learn to take great care of our energy as well as learn how to create boundaries around our ability to feel what others are feeling so that we can experience the world with sensitivity but, without being overwhelmed.

In mediumship, it can be a slippery slope to allow the self to be in empath mode. Think about it for a minute. When you are an empath, you personally take on the feelings and energies of people or places around you, as if they were your own. In mediumship, it is likely that most of the people who sit with you will be in various stages of grief and loss, and of course with that comes lower vibrational energy. In order to receive and blend well with spirit, we must be a close vibrational match to them – otherwise, the blend or merge will not occur. Our energy and spirits will be like oil and water – no blending! And so if you are allowing yourself to remain in empath mode while working in mediumship, you will plummet your own vibrational frequency and blending with spirit will be weak, intermittent, or impossible.

One of the wonders of being empathic is that it can help to sensitize us to the experiences of others, creating greater levels of compassion and understanding within oneself. The ability to identify with others in this way is a super-power. It helps us all to remain connected to one another, to experience unity, and it allows us to step into true and deep compassion. And so while being empathic needs to be controlled within the context of giving a mediumship reading, you are also encouraged to experience the world around you through empathic means, because the gift is within you for a reason, least of which is to share your ability to connect so deeply with others so they may feel seen and understood.

Learning to control your empathic nature is essential as a medium. You must learn to allow the energy of others to penetrate your own energy field in order to know their experience as needed, but additionally learn to not allow it in. Instead, give yourself permission to stay separate from the energy of others as needed to preserve your own wellness, as it does not serve anyone to let your energy get dragged down simply because we are unwittingly attuning to others.

The Compassionate Observer

Rather than allow yourself to be empathically present for your clients and risk bottoming-out your energy field (thereby negatively impacting your mediumship abilities), consider developing your ability to serve as a Compassionate Observer. The compassionate observer is a state of being or perspective in which we interact with the client without judgment, with a tender heart and soft ear, really seeing them, but doing so without taking on their current experience of grief and loss as your own. See beyond the damage, and into their soul – in all its glory. This position is very helpful to practice especially when delivering a reading for someone who is in very deep grief. Please remember to maintain the softness of seeing them and offering comfort, but do not become them and their experience.

Psychic Mode in Mediumship: Pitfalls and Blessings

What is the difference between a psychic and a medium? Being psychic is having (or developing) the ability to perceive information about people, places, objects, and situations through special means. The information is perceived by the psychic through energy. It is important you understand that all people, places, things, and situations have consciousness or soul or essence and therefore hold (or more accurately, are) information. Being psychic is the ability to understand that information in terms of energy rather than understanding or knowing it through traditional means. Psychic skills include the clairsenses (clairvoyance, clairaudience, clairsentience, claircognizance). These clair abilities or psychic skills are how we become aware of information available in the field of energy around us. The psychic skills are also how we become aware of information being communicated to us by spirit people. And therein lies the difference. As psychics, we perceive information available in the field of energy around us. As mediums, we receive information from another soul. There is a being, an active participant, at the other end of the communication in mediumship, whereas there is no other being communicating to us in psychic work. In psychic work, we are simply becoming aware of information that is present and available to be known.

The psychic vibrational frequency is lower than that of mediumship, and so it is much easier for people to reach this vibration than it is to reach the mediumship frequency. I often work with students who have come from another teacher at some point in their training, and sometimes they will tell me they have been trained to drop down to psychic frequency rather than receiving information from spirit if they are not getting much information from a spirit person at the start of a reading. However, there is a plethora of reasons not to do this. First, if you step down and get comfortable in psychic mode, it will likely take you a fair amount of time before reaching the mediumship frequency again within the same reading. Instead, you might consider working in a much more focused way in order to reach the vibrational frequency you need in order to connect with spirit, right from the get-go.

If you cannot perceive a spirit person, you may not have prepared yourself appropriately. There are times that, despite your best effort, you may not be at the optimal vibration. Go back into your meditative state, and spend a little more time preparing yourself internally by relaxing your body, clearing your mind, clearing your personal energy, and expanding your auric field. Then ask for the connection with spirit, again. If it does not happen, it may be because you are not feeling well, you may be overly tired, or you may be really distracted by something in your life. Be kind to yourself. Allow yourself to have off days every so often, but do not go into psychic mode in the meantime if your client is seeing you for a mediumship reading. If someone has come to you for a mediumship reading, they may not want a psychic reading, and in fact may become upset if you tune in to their personal energy field and learn about them. Instead, call it a day, and try again when you feel you are ready.

If you offer both psychic and mediumship readings combined (and many do, including me), consider structuring the session by holding the mediumship part of the reading first, followed by the psychic part. It can be difficult to start in psychic mode and then have to shift upwards, vibrationally, while you are sitting with someone. It is much easier to 'drop down' from medium mode to psychic mode than to shift up from psychic to medium.

Chapter Four

Moving Beyond Raw Skill: Personal Development

§

As you spend more time working as a medium – professionally, or not — there will be times that your raw ability to channel a spirit person will not be enough to shift someone, as we have discussed. Their grief or circumstances might be affecting them so strongly that, despite being an excellent medium, your reading was not enough to make them feel any differently or any better. In such situations, we have two choices: 1. Accept that we may not be the person to help them on their journey at this time, and that is always okay. Or, 2. Provide them with a higher level of service, one that touches the soul in a totally different way. The way to up the level of service you offer begins by helping ourselves and leading ourselves through the places we hope to lead others. Tending to our own wounds, fears, and limitations in belief, is the essence of soul-based work. It is absolutely essential to address our own situations on a continuous basis in becoming and growing as a great medium.

The journey toward becoming a medium can be a very exciting one — filled with first-time, mind and soul altering experiences. After all, coming to know the unseen world in personal and passionate ways is fascinating and unique, and no one's pathway is ever quite the same.

Along the road we take classes, workshops, seek out mentors, read volumes of books, and venture on many roads-less-traveled in search of powerful connections to ourselves, the spirit world, and the universe at large. One thing however, that we can sometimes miss, is the call from within to tend to blocks and woundedness inside our very selves. We can sometimes be so motivated to help the other — to find ways to ease the suffering and spur the growth and healing of those who might need our help, that we miss the very first and most crucial aspect of any spiritual work: healing the self.

As intermediary between the worlds, mediums have the honour and privilege of relaying messages of importance from those in spirit to those here in the living. But along with that ever-important task, the vocation carries with it tremendous responsibility to get it right. But what does getting it right even mean? Through teaching, I have consistently found tremendous value, and in fact necessity, to move beyond just the skill development aspects of mediumship. The development of greater levels of one's own soul-consciousness (you could also think of this as becoming more spirit-like) has to be preceded by some level of healing within the personality or ego bodies.

Guiding students to explore their own wounds, in search of meaning and eventual healing should probably be as much a part of the long-term syllabus in mediumship development as are exercises and experiences with spirit people. Healing is a big word though, and it can get lost in a sentence quite easily. What exactly is meant by 'healing'? The word itself needs to be understood more clearly, and in order to achieve that, we must break it down, and unpack it a little.

Healing is about extracting the knowledge that is available to you from a negative or wounding experience, and then integrating that knowledge and the ways it has benefited you, into your life in a meaningful way. Beyond the wounding itself, the process of healing really begins when we are able to assign or identify some meaning or larger purpose or usefulness behind the challenges. In order to discover meaning and purpose and eventually enter into the healing, we must touch the wound. We must find it, and we must come to know it honestly — deep as ever.

This is the part of personal development that can be scary — because it can hurt. But with the right guidance or mentorship from a coach, counsellor, or other trusted and soul-conscious individual or professional, you can absolutely enter into the woundedness and shift into healing. It is a beautiful universal truth and promise that following the darkness, we will enter into light. But we must truly and authentically confront that darkness, taking with us all there is to learn and know about the experience — no by-passing, no short-cuts. Walking through the mud is a good way to think of it...but the mud will eventually lead you to solid ground if you keep going.

We all have the choice to walk through the dark and make our way to the light, but conversely, we can also enter into the shadows and choose (consciously or unconsciously) to not walk through to the other side – into the knowledge, the freedom, and the growth. Each of us has the free will to choose as we please. And may we never judge the choices of others, but rather see them (and ourselves) as we are - full of truth, beauty, and goodness.

Within the context of mediumship, shadow and wound work holds much relevance. When spirit people transmit messages, the messages are usually two-tiered in that they touch two levels of a reality; they touch the specific or particular and form aspects of a reality, and they are also steeped in the universal aspects of a reality – also referred to as a greater reality than what the form world so easily perceives.

Spirit messages at the surface can be specific and pertinent, and often very resourceful in nature. For example, "Getting let go from your job was necessary and essential for you, even though you cannot see how it is beneficial from your current viewpoint. A new opportunity will await you once you have done a little more processing of the anger and fear that surfaced after you lost your job. Consider being open to opportunities presented to you by a close female friend." Behind (or more accurately, above) the resourceful message will be a universal truth being communicated. Strip away the details, and what is the spirit person saying? Filtered upward into a universal nature or theme, this message is stating a number of universal realities that need to be communicated, some of which could include:

1. All that we experience holds meaning and purpose, even if we cannot identify what they are right away or at all while still incarnate.

2. Doors will close that are not meant for us.

3. Doors will open when the timing is right and appropriate for us.

4. There is no blame to be issued, and the consciousness of blame is heavy and non-life-affirming.

5. While we have experiences within a life that are pre-planned by the soul, we also have free-will choice. This means that certain experiences will not come into our earthly life unless and until we have met other factors, which we reach through our own conscious choices to move forward and look at something with a deeper, more soul-infused lens.

6. Perceived negative experiences (wounds) highlight within us our own shadow - the parts of our soul consciousness that are not active, not identified with. In this way, woundedness is a powerful experience that points us in the direction of where we need to grow - it shows us our own shadow that is asking to be illuminated by the light of soul - it shows

us parts of our soul that we are disconnected from and not identified with.

7. All woundedness teaches us to stop relying on others to fulfill the needs of our soul and empowers us to self-generate the qualities we want and need to experience. This puts us in a power position in our own life rather than in a victim consciousness. Because of this, we can and may eventually be grateful for the wound. And if we do not arrive to this space of gratitude, that is always, always, always, ok. We are here to experience life in form. Learning and healing in the truest reality, are not requisites of a well-lived life. As a basic statement, life is about experiencing, it is not about learning necessarily. Our souls have infinity to evolve, and learning, evolving, processing and healing from a life can occur while alive or when we are back in spirit. There is no need to rush.

Would you believe it that in the message that was specifically about being fired, spirit would wanted you to say all of this, too? Well, they do, indeed. Souls in the otherworld are conscious beyond what we here in the physical world can perpetually obtain while still influenced by and expressing through physical bodies. The vibrational frequency of a transitioned spirit person far exceeds what we can achieve for any considerable length of time while in form. Their consciousness or lens through which they 'see' things is always one of knowingness, lovingness, and power, and as such, they want to impart this level of insight and wisdom to their loved ones here in the physical world. Why? Because they want to help us in our struggles as much as they can.

This leads us to our own growth, healing, and understanding of the nature of spirit and the universe at large. Because spirit people wish to have universal truths and realities communicated to their loved ones here in the physical, and we as mediums have made a commitment to serve in the role of messenger, then we must be equipped to share the messages we receive without distorting or filtering them.

If we do not tend to our own personal work throughout the journey of mediating between the two worlds, then we will have no personal understanding of universal truths to enhance our ability to communicate and truly understand what we hear and relay. If we have no lived experience, then how will we be able to communicate truth to someone else? If we have not successfully walked through some level of wounding to healing ourselves, how can we help lead someone else there, authentically?

There is a case to be made for any individual walking into hurt and pain for the purposes of emerging more empowered, more loving, more understanding, and more soul conscious. Becoming greater versions of ourselves is one of the gifts we can give ourselves during the earth walks we choose. The case is of even greater importance for those who wish to be the messengers for the other side.

Chapter Five

Real Life Challenges

§

The world of spirit is infinite. Infinity, of course, is impossible to map and know fully. So while we can become very much accustomed to and knowledgeable about the ways of the spirit world and after-death communication, nothing is ever exactly the same, 100% of time. There are always exceptions, which means that sometimes, things just do not go as planned and we cannot know the reason. And other times, things can go off-track and we can identify why and sometimes are able to remedy the situation.

Two common challenges that may arise in readings include:

1. A desired loved one on the other side does not make an appearance.
2. The information coming in is choppy and seems to cut in and out – the connection with spirit feels weak or faint.

What can be done when these problem present themselves?"

I can probably count on two hands how many times in thousands of private readings a desired loved one did not show up to communicate. It is not an overly common occurrence for a professional medium, but still, it can happen. What is happening when someone your client wants to hear from does not show up for the conversation? In my experience, there are usually three or four potential reasons for this. The first (and most common) is that only a short period of time may have passed since the spirit person's transition. All spirit people are different and assimilate, heal, learn, recover, etc. in different ways and in different timelines (using our sense of time, that is), And sometimes, when a person sits with a medium to have after-death communication, the loved one they want to hear from may not yet be ready to reach beyond the veil and in to contact with the medium. In my years as a professional, I have experienced the full spectrum of how long it takes a spirit person to become available for communication, from one day following transition to several years. We cannot fully know why or how each spirit person's journey is different; all we can know is that it is.

A few years ago, my maternal aunt transitioned to the spirit world unexpectedly. I learned she had passed the night that she transitioned and the following morning was scheduled to teach a mediumship development circle. I felt compelled to still hold the class, knowing that my aunt may want to make a public appearance, so to speak. Sure enough, she came through loud and clear through one of the students (I had not disclosed to the students what had occurred the prior evening, which made this particular experience incredibly powerful and validating). I thought to myself, wow Aunt Tina, you were available so quickly! How amazing. Then, the following day, I checked in on her, myself. I wanted to know how she was doing. And when I reached out to her in spirit, it was very clearly shown to me that she was not available for communication. Specifically, my spirit guides showed me that she was in a cocoon, and I understood she was doing some healing work related to the life she had just come from. It was fascinating to me that she was so available, so communicative, so clear, on the day after she passed. And then one day later, totally unavailable. I share this story to teach you one of the possible realities at play in mediumship, and in this case specifically, that spirit often becomes available for communication immediately after their passing simply to let the family know they are okay and that they (their soul) survived. And in quick order following the transmission of that message, they can 'go offline' or become unavailable for communication until a later date.

Sometimes there were misdeeds or misgivings between the spirit person and your client. There may have been words left unsaid, or your client may be angry or disappointed in the spirit person for any number of reasons. If there was friction in the relationship, is it possible that the spirit person may hesitate to connect because they do not want to force communication on your client? Absolutely. And this happens more often than you might think. The spirit may come to you slowly, barely discernible, and feeling very quiet. As you slowly present them in this type of circumstance, they tend to begin with an apology or an acknowledgment of how your sitter is feeling about them. Once they see your client is receptive to hearing from them, the floodgates of communication open. Conversely, if your sitter is not receptive to hearing from them, spirit will cease to communicate with you. And other times still, if the spirit person has not processed some difficult parts of their life, they may not be ready to communicate with your sitter.

I remember a reading where I had brought through an uncle, a grandmother, and a friend's mother who were all very clearly recognized by my client. Three quarters of the way through the session, my client indicated to me that she was happy to hear from the spirit people who had stepped forward, but that there was one more person with whom she was really hoping to connect. Given the limited time we had left, I used a technique called "Calling by Name" (more on this later). Upon doing this, I had only the faintest sense of another, new spirit with me. He was so faint, you could almost miss his presence, entirely. I tried to gain any information I could from him, but the most I got back was that he had a sudden and unexpected departure, and his mother was still here in the physical world. Both of these points, however basic, were validated as true. Following this, he began to issue an apology to his mom, and he let me know his mom was disappointed in him for life choices he had made, especially related to his family, which I understood from him included two children and a partner/wife at some point. This too was validated as true. Next, he began to apologize to my client who I understood from him at that point was one of his children, his daughter. Once I brought this information through and my client emotionally connected with her father's spirit, his spirit began to communicate strongly. It was like night and day how hesitant he was to begin with, not knowing if his daughter was alright hearing from him. But once her willingness to connect became clear, his spirit relayed lots of information.

Another possible reason for a loved one not making an appearance, even though they may be fully assimilated in the spirit world, is actual, physical-world time constraints. As mediums, we typically have a defined period of time within which we sit with someone for a reading. The durations of time may be anywhere from 20-60 minutes or even longer sometimes. And every so often, if a client has a long list of people in the spirit world, or if the energy of a desired loved one is not as strong as other spirits, then we could reach the end of a reading having not brought through the one person from whom our client wanted to hear. As professionals, how can we do better in situations such as this?

Here is how and it is a quick and simple solution:

Midway through your reading, be sure to check in with your client that there is not someone else they would also like to hear from. I typically phrase the question this way: "Are you happy to stay with this spirit person, or are there others you might like to hear from?" Using this language gives you a greater opportunity to connect with potentially other spirit people your client would really like to hear from. Unsure about how to move from one spirit person to another? More on that shortly.

Another experience that occurs from time to time, even in advanced or professional mediumship, is information coming in a choppy way, and the connection with spirit feels weak or faint. A few reasons can lie behind this phenomenon. First, when a spirit person is transitioned and assimilated to the spirit world, I have found that there can be varying degrees of assimilation, including varying degrees of knowing how to communicate without a body anymore. If someone was recently transitioned but still able to make contact with you as a medium, sometimes their ability to communicate clearly is just not there yet. They may not be able to hold the energy and hold the blend with you for any appreciable length of time. And this is what can cause information to feel like it is coming in choppy or faint. If this is the reason behind the weak connection, there is not much you can do to change it, other than to suggest to your client to make a return visit once a little more time has passed.

Another reason information can be choppy or the connection can feel faint is your own preparation as a medium. Did you spend enough time clearing your energy and the energy of your space? Did you spend enough time relaxing and meditating ahead of time? The most common reason behind a weak connection is the medium's lack of quality preparation time. The good news is that if this happens to you in a reading, you can always go silent for a few minutes and hit the reset button. Get centered, relaxed, and clear, and call spirit to you once more.

Rounding out the possible reasons why a desired loved one may not make an appearance or the information coming through is choppy is, of course, that there is no apparent reason. The spirit world and its goings-on are vast and complex, and as humans in the physical world, we are not always able to comprehend it. Rest assured however, that not being able to determine the reason behind the challenges noted above will not occur very often, and it is more likely that you will be able to identify the reason for the challenge and address it in a satisfying and understandable way for your client.

Challenging Sitters

Contrary to what many people may believe, it is not uncommon for someone to sit with a medium and come with a closed energy field. One would think the willingness to have a reading would equal a very open energy on part of the sitter, but alas, this is not always the case!

If someone has booked an appointment to come and sit with you, you can assume they want to believe that the afterlife exists. But that does not mean they will be willing participants in the process of of witnessing it. They may have a reserved, prove-it-to-me attitude, which can have a negative impact on the process of mediumship. Before making any judgments about your sitter, it is good to know why people close their energy fields when sitting with a medium. One of the most common reasons is they may be in the anger stage of grief, and that anger may project out toward you for no good reason. Sometimes people are picky about who they want to hear from and remain incredibly closed off to hearing from anyone other than their one special person in spirit. Other times, your sitter is an inherent skeptic, and their prevailing attitude is one of general judgment, disbelief, and sometimes criticism.

So what do we do when faced with a sitter who is really closed off to connecting with you and the process? Remember, it is not your responsibility to prove anything, to anyone. Stay clear about your job, which is to relay information from the spirit world. How someone receives that information and what they do with it is totally out of your hands, and you have to be okay with that. Keeping this in mind will help prevent you from feeling like you have to perform for someone. If you inadvertently slip into this mindset, your vibrational frequency will lower because you are focusing on yourself rather than on service, and this will cause your auric field to shrink. And from there, like a domino effect, your ability to stay blended with spirit will diminish and the quality and quantity of information will be reduced, thereby fulfilling the very scenario you were afraid of in the first place! Moral of the lesson: stay in your power. It is also totally okay and totally appropriate to let your sitter know their energy feels closed off, and to get as much information/clarity as possible, they could help by trying to relax. This is to shift their energy into one of loving connection, which will help in the three-way process between your sitter, spirit, and yourself.

During your opening speech at the beginning of your readings, you will want to let your sitter know that many spirits may come to you, not just the ones they would like to hear from. This can help prepare them for the possibility that the desired loved one may not make an appearance right away (or at all), and knowing this ahead of time can help keep the sitter from shutting down. And this leads us to the next level of mediumship progression – the ability to move from one spirit person to another within one reading. As a professional, you will want to be able to shift, at will, from spirit to spirit to ensure a higher likelihood of your sitter hearing from who they want to hear from in the spirit world. In my very early mediumship days, I would accept the first person in spirit who came to me. I would ask them all the questions in my framework, and that was it. I would not look for another person to bring through, and if the person I connected with was not at the top of my sitter's desired loved ones list, I would chalk it up to spirit choosing who was speaking that day. And while that is ultimately true – spirit does determine who shows up – it is also true that as mediums, we can run out of time in a reading before the desired loved one has a chance to make it through to us. Certainly, you will want to avoid this in professional mediumship as much as is practicable. So be sure to check in with your sitter throughout your reading. It is not uncommon for me to ask my sitter, "Is this someone you would like to connect with today?" or, "Would you like me to stay with this loved one, or would you like me to see who else is with us?" Some readings can turn out to be like huge parties on the other side, and you may bring through five to ten spirits in one sitting! And at other times, there will only be one or two. Engage with your sitter to understand what would be most helpful to them during their time with you. And then to the best of your ability, provide that for them while maintaining the integrity of your work. So, how do we move from one spirit to another, at will? Hang tight. It is coming up next.

Chapter Six

Navigating Spirits

§

By now you may have experienced what it feels like to move from one spirit to another in a reading, and if you have, it has likely been because one spirit stepped back and another stepped forward. You may have even experienced a shift in spirit people without being aware it occurred, until the information suggested that you shifted from one spirit to the next. You may have given many points of validation demonstrating one spirit in particular and it all made perfect sense to your sitter. Then, a new and specific piece of information does not make sense to the sitter as something coming from the original spirit person. Rather, it makes absolute sense for another spirit. For example, you may be bringing through someone's dear friend and the reading is going very well. Then, the next piece of validation is that their dear friend traveled a lot, specifically to somewhere in the United Kingdom, Ireland you believe it is, to fish. Your sitter may reply, "No, my friend never did that, but my dad did." Following this, another piece of information comes through that also makes sense for their dad, and you continue on in this trend for three or more points of validation. This is your cue that you have, in fact, moved to another spirit person. It did not occur at your will but rather at the spirit's will. And we must honour and allow that to happen when it does. Sometimes, we can even make our way back to the original spirit if it is desired that we do so.

Shifting by choice from one spirit to another is a skill that takes some practice, so if you have not already started to do this, make it a point to start practicing. I like to describe making the shift this way; in your mind's eye, go out looking. Search the spaces in your mind. Look beyond where you were focused with the first spirit person. Set the intention that you are connecting with a new spirit, and go looking for one in your mind.

Another approach to shifting from one spirit to another is calling a spirit by name. This technique is useful if you have a short period of time to bring through someone important for your sitter. For example, you may be doing a very brief, fifteen minute reading at a trade show, or you may have a client who arrived very late for their appointment and you only have twenty minutes with them. Otherwise, I do not advise calling for spirit by name in any other circumstances. A major validating factor in evidential mediumship is bringing a spirit person through and demonstrating their existence without any information from your sitter, whatsoever.

Calling by name is as it sounds. You will ask your sitter for the name of someone they would like to hear from in the spirit world. And then, in your mind, call out that name by projecting an announcement into the field, looking for the spirit who matches the name, and is connected to your sitter. In my mind, it sounds like this, "Carol connected to Louise, step forward. I invite you to me as my friend. Carol, connected to Louise, come sit with me." You might like to use similar wording in your own practice. Please note that calling by name is not a guarantee that you will receive the spirit you are looking for, but it certainly has the potential to connect you quickly to a specific spirit person, and by-pass any others who might be present. When a spirit person presents to me after calling by name, I will typically begin presenting to my client by saying, "Okay, you can let me know if this sounds like [name of spirit person]..." Even though I have called for spirit by name, I make no assumptions that the spirit person presenting to me is the person I have called. The information itself should do that - the information has to be correct for that person. And sometimes it is not. And that is okay. Sometimes the person you bring through after calling by name is a different loved one belonging to your sitter. In this situation, I may try once more, or I may say to my client, "This is who we have coming through right now, and there is not much I can do about that." Typically your sitter will be understanding of the fact that you tried to make the contact they were looking for.

Sometimes there are other reasons to move from one spirit to another. Though your intention as a medium is to connect with souls who have transitioned to the spirit world, you may come into contact with a grounded or un-transitioned spirit. Grounded spirits, or lower energy spirits as they are sometimes referred to, or even ghosts sometimes, are earthbound souls, or discarnate beings, who died but have not managed to get to the other side. They are usually attached in some way to the form world, whether it is a person, a place, an object. They may feel a very strong allegiance, which compels them to protect someone, something, or a place, or they may simply feel a proprietary protectiveness. Other times, they may not know that their body has died and the soul is free from form to carry on in the soul journey. Disorientation occurs on occasion, which can cause a spirit person to be confused and truly unaware that their physical body has indeed died. Now, you might think this kind of thing (making contact with a ghost) only happens when visiting old places, or abandoned buildings, or spooky locations with historical significance, but that simply is not true. Lower energy spirits, or ghosts, can be attached to the people you read for. How will you recognize a lower energy spirit in a reading? I think the best way to describe what they feel like is by describing what they *do not* feel like. Think of a wise old grandma in the spirit world – loving, beautiful, and radiating light. Grounded spirits will not feel like this. They will feel quite the opposite – cold and odd. They may be very quiet in their communication, or sometimes they are very, very opinionated about something. As soon as you recognize a spirit is communicating to you about a polarized opinion they have, this will be a good clue that you are in contact with a ghost, and not a transitioned spirit.

I have had more experiences than I can count in a mediumship reading where a loved one, connected directly to my client, did not make their transition to the spirit world and when they presented to me, were of a lower vibration.

Now as a medium, you have two options if and when this happens to you. First, do as we have discussed above and shift over to another spirit. There is nothing wrong with doing this. If you are unable and untrained to assist a grounded spirit with their journey, then there is simply nothing for you to offer them. And that is okay. They will eventually make their own way, or someone else may assist them. If you encounter a spirit who feels to be of a lower vibration in your reading, my suggestion is to not indulge in communication. If you do, the un-transitioned spirit may attach to you as they are likely to feel some comfort or validation of their presence because you are aware of them. While this is an undesirable situation, it is not the end of the world, but you will need to remove the attachment or have it removed for you.

Your second option, if you feel powerful enough in your own energy and have a total absence of fear for the subject matter, is to offer assistance to the grounded spirit. Before we begin this part of your training, make note that my recommendation is that you seek out a mentor to assist you in your continued development in spirit rescue or releasement. Indeed, an entire book could be dedicated to the practice of assisting grounded spirits, but we will begin your learning in this chapter as a starting point in your advanced mediumship practice.

Releasing a spirit person who has stayed with you after a session can be quite easy to deal with in some cases, but in others, much more difficult. To start, you need to give the act of assisting a spirit to release from the physical world the time that it needs. There can be no rushing through. The act must be thorough, even if that means it takes twice as long as you would like.

The spirit person may or may not be communicative with you. Perhaps, you may observe them observing you. If they are communicative, you will want to engage in an empowered dialogue with them, explaining to them their scenario (that they have passed from the physical world) and what awaits them when they release their attachment to this space and time. We may assure them that the universal is all loving. We will let them know there is no benefit for them to remain within this space, and we may ask for the assistance of beings of light such as angels or spirit guides to come greet them. This dialogue may go on for some time, and you must allow the time it takes because you can not force it. They must make the choice themselves. This does not mean beings of light can not assist them — indeed they do. But spirit, just as we do in physical form, has free will choice. What does this mean as it relates to you as a medium? It means you may not be successful at releasing a spirit because the spirit may choose not to be released. In these cases, you may attempt contact again at a later date, you might ask for assistance from another professional, or you may simply let it go from your task list (so long as the spirit is not attached to you, personally.) If an un-transitioned spirit stays with you after a reading, try to deal with the situation straight away; it will likely be an easier task to release them if they have not been with you for an extended period.

In your empowered dialogue, you may discover the spirit has requests, and sometimes you can oblige them, and sometimes you simply cannot. For example, I remember doing an energy clearing at an historic building that was haunted by a long-gone caretaker of the building. In my communication with him, he asked me who would take care of the place if not him. He also asked if the current curator of the building would look after its interests long term. And so, I asked would she take care of the place so the old caretaker could release from his self-imposed perpetual duties of looking after the building. And only when she answered me, in a very committed way, that she would be a steward of the building so long as she was there, would the old caretaker sever his cord from the place and move on with his soul's journey.

When we cannot oblige their requests, we simply need to reassure them that all will be okay, and that the form world will evolve as it needs. Informing them that they can no longer influence the world of form is a very powerful piece of information for a ghost to process. Often, it is a pivotal moment where they reconsider their conscious or unconscious decision to stay attached to the earth plane. Another powerful part of the process is to call for help from the angels, guides, and other helping spirits. These beings of light should be part of the practice of spirit rescue, each and every time. It is often an additionally helpful part of the process to invite in loved ones from the other side who are related to the un-transitioned spirit. Facilitating a reunion-of-sorts can be an ensuring way to encourage the grounded spirit to release themselves from the earth plane and make their way to the other side. Asking the light beings for direct assistance in the soul's ascension is also not out of the question. Sometimes, there are means beyond our understanding that come into play to help a spirit transition, and you may feel you are a passive observer of the process unfolding in front of you. You may visualize this process in any way that feels fitting. Do not stop your process until you have a deep certainty that the energy has been moved and is being taken care of, and is no longer in your space or your personal energy field. Fill yourself and the entire space with light, and give thanks for any help given. Finally, as is the case after any spiritual work, follow it up by clearing the self and space fully, and grounding yourself. Eat, walk around, go outside, connect back to your physical body.

If you encounter an un-transitioned spirit in a reading and the spirit belongs to your client, you will have to take special care in sharing with your client what is going on. They generally are okay hearing their loved one is still doing their healing work and assimilating. And it is okay to tell them this is what is happening with their loved one, and as such, they may not be available (or fully available) for communication. Clients might, however, worry and even become scared if we tell them their loved one has not transitioned - especially if we were not able to help their loved one through to the next phase of their soul's journey. So, if you experience a lower vibration and you feel you need to share it, simply let your client know their spirit loved one is still doing their soul work. In fact, no matter what the circumstances, the truth is they are still doing their soul work, and it is okay to share this.

Chapter Seven

Personal Protection and Clearing Energy

§

As energy workers, we perpetually find ourselves working within the energy fields of other people, places, and objects. Even though our intention in mediumship is to connect with transitioned spirits, we may also encounter spirits who have not transitioned and are grounded to the earth plane. We are also sensitive to vibrations even when we are not working. Often, we consciously and intentionally come face-to-face with lower frequencies and so, in order to protect ourselves from being bombarded by those lower energies, we must learn to manage our personal energy, including fear around this subject matter, for the purpose of avoiding an unwanted spiritual intrusion. And, we must also learn how to manage a personal intrusion, should one occur.

Everyone has the power to change the quality of an energy using personal power, divine power, or earth power, combined with intention and with or without the use of tools. Energy from the formless is constantly flowing into the world of form and back out again because energy is always in a state of motion. And universal energy can be shaped by our thoughts and feelings. The process works like this: As universal energy passes through us in its perpetual cycle of motion, our thoughts and feelings shape the energy (or add a quality to it). The energy eventually moves out of form again, but before it does so, it is filtered through our form selves (physical, mental, emotional bodies.) As such, when the energy moves back into formlessness, it is imbued with our energy. What was generally neutral energy now has very specific qualities – positive and negative, or higher and lower energy.

Most people do not tend to their own personal energy fields and have no idea what they are putting out into the universe. This reality means there are all kinds of lower-quality formless energies floating around us all the time, and we can and will experience these non-beneficial energies in the universe at some point. These energies can manifest within a person, place, or thing, and animate the host. Have you ever met someone, held an object, or visited a place that just rubbed you the wrong way because it felt negative, or gave you the creeps? You may have encountered a lower energy that attached itself to that person, place, or thing. Lower energies can also be transient and unattached to anything and may simply float around or stick to things, including you and others, along its perpetual cycle of motion.

While there is no gold stamp of certainty, the greatest defense against a spiritual intrusion, whether you are working or not, is to keep your own vibration high. You can maintain a high quality energy field for yourself by doing the following:

1. Monitoring and managing the quality of your thoughts;
2. Cultivating thoughts and beliefs that connect with greater realities and universal truths;
3. Consciously living the message of spirit;
4. Continuing to expose the shadows within for the purposes of learning, healing, and growing, thereby bringing the unconscious to the conscious, or the dark into the light;

5. Committing to knowing, accepting, and loving the self, in all of its positive and negative aspects;
6. Continuing to cultivate the power of heart and connection to soul, in order to live more fully from the heart;
7. Checking in often with the higher self;
8. Checking in with guides and helpers along the journey, especially at decision-making times. The check-in is to listen openly to the self or spirit about whether or not something is right for you. The ego can easily interfere. Learn to pause and listen;
9. Self-care in all its aspects – rest, high vibration food intake, taking soul time, meditation, flow time, nature time, high vibration company, smiling, laughing, lightness. Remember not to take yourself too seriously!
10. Focusing on appreciation and gratitude and expressing both, often.

One thing I have learned about working with the world of spirit is that anything is possible, at any time. And so you may implement and actively practice all of the above suggestions, and still, you may experience an intrusion. So then what? You might start by asking, how will I know if I am experiencing a spiritual intrusion either after working with a client or at any time? The first task in order to identify an intrusion within your own field is to get to know your own energy intimately so you can sense when something does not belong to you. You have to know what is you, so you can identify the presence of an energy that is *not* you.

When you know what being you feels like, it will be easy to recognize when you feel out of sorts, in terms of your energy. One exercise I like to do after any session with a client is scanning my energy field, using visualization through my mind's eye. I visualize a grid over myself, and systematically scan through each section of the grid for anything unusual. This exercise can and should be practiced often. Allow yourself the time you need, and allow yourself to become aware of anything that seems to not belong in your energy field. We can also call in our helpers, whether guides, guardians, protectors or animal spirits to help us in the discovery intrusions. When, however, we are in spiritual danger, these spiritual helpers will often just appear to assist if we have already cultivated a relationship with them. Now what do we do with whatever we find? We are getting there.

We each have natural storehouses of life-force energies throughout our bodies, and one of these locations is in your lower belly, three thumb widths down from the navel and three thumb widths inward. This energy centre has been referred to as the lower Dantian, the Sei-ka Tanden, or the Hara. When we are dealing with potentially very low energies, we will want to expand our own personal power by focusing on this energy centre and then increasing it.

Building Power from Within

An Exercise for Expanding Personal Energy

Life energy is moved by the mind. To focus on the energy centres of power is to place one's energy there. As we each focus on growing our individual energy centres, we begin placing ourselves in our own powerful glory and soul-essence. It is through focus and intention that we are powering ourselves up to our highest energetic potential.

Now, sit down and settle your mind. Close your eyes, and relax your body. Bring your focus and attention to that area in your lower belly. Take a soft and long breath into this area. As you inhale, visualize that the power of this centre is expanding. With each breath, your power is increasing. Stand up now, and plant your feet, shoulder-width apart, on to the ground. Now stomp your feet on the ground. Feel the energetic ripple moving out from you. With each stomp, your own energy, so powerful, reverberates all around. Feel that power, and own it. Stand in it. It is all yours. Once you have experienced this power, sit back down, come back into your body. But always remember what it felt like. Repeat this exercise often.

Sometimes, we work with individuals either here or on the other side who exist at a lower vibration. Sometimes this vibration causes a fear response of needing to protect ourselves from them. When working with very damaged clients or spirits, we may become nervous that their energy will contaminate us, and we let fear in. Instead of working from a place of fear, we can go further into their energy to that place of soul energy, and see their power and beauty and love. The damaged parts are only one portion of who they truly are. It is important not to shift to a place of fear, but rather operate from a place of powerful observation that also sees the soul within them. When you truly see their souls, you are seeing the larger part of them, made of power, love, and intelligence, but from which they have become disconnected. The damage at the surface and in deeper levels that you are aware of is real. But so too are the dormant qualities of truth, beauty, and goodness common among all beings.

Even still, there will be times when you will not want to explore and witness the best dormant parts of a spirit or living person, and instead, you will want to be very clear in your boundary around your own well being or that of the people closest to you. For example, if you were to experience a low-energy spirit in your home and you are unable to assist in its release, that does not mean you should accept their continued presence in your home. Instead, you will, with deep determination and power, clear them from your home, even if it means they simply leave and take up residence somewhere else. You can only do what you are capable of doing, and when your own limitations prevent you from some aspect of spiritual work, taking care of yourself and the wellness of those closest to you will be what you focus on. And that is always alright.

For substantial energy intrusions, your run-of-the-mill energy clearing approaches like basic visualization of white light, burning herbs, using reiki energy, etc. are often not enough. With substantial intrusions, it is important to make contact with the intrusion, either by yourself or through the assistance of someone who can approach the situation without fear. Personal power is essential in clearing, and we must not hold fear because it impedes our ability to be active, powerful and deliberate participants in the clearing. We are sometimes dealing with thoughtforms, which is energy infused by persistent negative thoughts or emotions, and this energy exists outside of the person with whom the thoughts or emotions originated. Thoughtforms, which are just as real and powerful as grounded spirits or ghosts, will try to avoid being noticed. When clearing these energies, just as with releasing grounded spirits, we must 'check' whether or not our actions were effective. When attempting to clear an intrusion, either in your own energy field or within a space, make no assumptions that what you have done has actually worked. When we just go through the motions of clearing without really focusing on the work and verifying the result, we may miss things. Ritualistic motions without intention, without attention, and without visualizing the process as it is taking place, have very little power and effect.

As a general methodology, we want to identify the intrusion in some kind of concrete way (usually more than just a feeling). Even when it is just a feeling, allow the intrusion to take on some kind of form that you can imagine. Or sometimes, the intrusion has such intelligence that you will perceive it the way it wants to be perceived. An example of allowing the intrusion to take shape in your mind might be visualizing the intrusion as an actual shape, with a color, or texture, a temperature, etc. Or you may allow it to take on any image. We must be able monitor the state of the intrusion as we are working on it so that we know when it has detached, and the most effective way to do this is to visualize it in form.

Sometimes there are lessons for us to learn from the intrusion – this is especially true when the intrusion teaches us something about our own personal energy field that attracted the intrusion in the first place. For example, if you have been particularly judgmental, an un-transitioned spirit person who tends to be judgmental themselves, may be attracted to your energy because they will get to experience the energy of judgment and express it themselves, through you. Other times, the intrusion is consciously or unconsciously seeking transmutation and has some level of intelligence that you might be able to help in that regard (spirit people will sometimes do this). Non-form energy of a lower vibrational quality will also grow when fed with additional lower vibrational energy like fear. So if you hold much fear, it is like a good little meal ticket for persistent low quality energy.

Entity attachments are generated by human thoughts that have been infused with emotion and sometimes, with intent. Astral entities more or less float around in the ether and can latch on to someone who is vulnerable, overly open, or fatigued. They typically attach to something within you that is a frequency match, and these entities often appear as gray/black blobs but they can take on shape (including very pleasant or unpleasant imagery).

A ghost, or an earthbound soul who died but has not managed to get to the other side, is typically identified with and attached to the earth plane, usually because of a strong connection to a place, event, or person. These beings can connect to our energy field when there is some link between us and them (for example, if you are a medium working with someone connected to them), and they can also be drawn to our light, as mediums.

Of all of these different types of attachments we can find in our own energy fields, some have never been in human form and are just negative thought bodies that have attached themselves to us. In all of these potential cases of attachments in our energy, in our spaces, or in our objects, they are taking up valuable space and are creating a negative impact on our lives. They must be removed. Some pretty dramatic personality shifts can occur once these energies are released.

Visualization is a very important aspect of energy clearing. It is setting the intention for the work that must be done and visualizing the process that is to take place. Ringing singing bowls or burning palo santo are just actions until you add visualization and intention to the process. You must be both the action and the intention as you do the work of clearing.

An Exercise

Clearing the Energy in a Room or Your Own Personal Energy Field

Close your eyes and begin viewing the room or your own energy field through your psychic sight. Begin by visualizing the room or your aura around you. Scan the space or yourself, energetically. Visualize or allow for your mental faculties to cloak vibrational information in such a way that you will notice it. Often lower vibration will catch your attention fleetingly and you can scan past it. I offer you this information so that you will always pay attention to even the smallest indication of lower energy that catches your attention - even if it looks pleasant. On a number of occasions while clearing the energy fields of other people and places, I have encountered intrusions that look like smiley-face emojis in my mind. At first glance, these images may be interpreted as neutral or positive. However, upon further investigation, and each and every time, these intrusions had sufficient intelligence to try to evade my awareness and thus trespass in a person's energy field where they did not belong.

Tune in to any areas or anything at all that catches your attention. Do not be fooled. Fear may kick in here, but hold on to your power. The power of your form body is so substantial, and you do not have anything to be afraid of.

Breathe into and expand the energy centre below your navel if you feel it is necessary to stay out of fear. Now observe something about this presence – do you get a sense of it as a whole being such as a discarnate being, or a non-whole being such as a remnant of energy, or a thoughtform? Note that not all intrusions will be felt as 'low vibration' – they may feel quite benign at this time, but in any case if they are unwanted, they need to be addressed.

If the intrusion energy is a spirit person who does not belong with you, you will follow the instructions in the chapter entitled, Navigating Spirits.

Now that you have identified the intrusion, it is time to clear it from yourself or your space. Begin by asking for help from spirit – your guides, helpers, the angels, helping spirits, the forces of light, and earth power if you so choose. Now through active, powerful, and intentional means, we must use visualization techniques in this empowered clearing not only to 'see' the intrusion, but to remove it. You may choose to use light, water (rain, waves, fire hose, etc.), vacuuming, burning, wind power, disintegrating thunder, lightning, swallowing by mother earth below to do the clearing. Visualize one or all of these powerful forces to release the energy from yourself or your space. This can sometimes take longer than you would like. Do not rush it. If it was a simple fix, then ringing singing bowls in your room would have worked. Continue to hold the power, and monitor the progress of the release. Keep at it, and change up the visualization tool if it feels necessary. I will often switch between water, air, light, fire, and soil within one energy clearing. I will also use the help of angels and helping spirits (usually power animals) to assist me.

Once the energy has been released, direct it toward transmutation by mother earth or the heavens, whichever feels appropriate. I have used both - directing the energy up to the heavens or down into mother earth once the energy has been released from its host (person, place, or thing). Wherever you direct it, you must have certainty that the energy has been moved and is being taken care of, and is no longer in your space or within your energy field. Fill the vacant space with light and then move outward and fill the entire space or body with light. Give thanks for all help given, and close the space by grounding yourself and making a return to ordinary reality.

Spiritual intrusions are not the only disturbances we might find in our energy fields that we need to be aware of. Energy strands are invisible — yet very real — lines of energy that connect us to people, places, and things. These strands, cords, or filaments that connect us can come from experiences in this life or even past lives, and they most often connect to us through one of our chakras, although there are exceptions.

Energy strands are not just the etheric cords of connection between people, events, places, and objects; they also serve as a pathway for subconsciously sending and receiving energy and information to and from the people, places, events, and objects around you. If you are not aware of the cords attached to you then you may receive a great deal of energy and information that does not belong to you. You may also receive a negative energy cord from someone who is thinking very negative thoughts about you.

You have strands to your parents, siblings, children, friends, partners, co-workers, and the list can go on. Additionally, strands form between you and your home and its objects, pets, past lives, ancestors, locales around the world where you have lived (in this life and others), houses you have lived in, your guides, angels, the universe, and even ideas and concepts. You do not live in isolation; you are being influenced and influencing the world around you every moment.

There are some tell-tale signs of heavy cording, and while many of these can also be attributed to other causes, they can indicate the presence of many corded attachments in your energy field.

1. Chronic Exhaustion;
2. New behavior patterns that you do not recognize as your own;
3. Random, unwanted thoughts;
4. Unhealthy attachments to people/places/things;
5. Aching for a past relationship;
6. Obsessive thoughts;
7. Depression and hopelessness.

Some questions to ask yourself when examining your own cording:

Do you subconsciously enjoy the feeling of being needed, even if needy people are depleting your energy? Do you need to be needed? Have you given your power away to someone in an effort for that person to like you? Has your need for approval overridden the needs of your soul? Do you have a dysfunctional relationship but choose to remain bound? Do you feel the need to rescue others because you wish to feel important? The law of attraction states that like attracts like, so how are you pulling these cords toward you?

It is imperative that you know your own energy field so that you can discern when something is affecting it. Do this work from a position of power – not from fear. Cords may have to be cut on a regular basis as many can re-connect. So it is important to continue to monitor them once cut so that you can tend to any that grow back. If a cord re-attaches, understand that this occurrence is showing you where some attention is needed in your own personal growth and development, and more understanding in relation to the cord and your own tendencies is needed. Once you know what has happened, the next step is to integrate that knowledge in to your life in a meaningful way — create the new version of yourself that comes from knowing what you know now. Be that new person. Once this occurs, the cord will never regenerate.

An Exercise
Cord Cutting

Prepare yourself by relaxing – light a candle, take a bath, listen to relaxing music, meditate, etc.

1) Sit in a quiet space and call on your spirit helpers to assist you;

2) Expand your own energy centres by breathing in to your chakras;

3) Begin by scanning your own energy field for any intrusive cords that may be attached;

4) If you find cords, you need to assess whether these cords need to be removed;

5) Ask yourself if this cord is for your highest and best life. If yes, then leave the cord. If not, you will want to detach it;

6) Visualize the cord to be cut and send loving kindness to the person, object, or place on the other end. We can cut cords and still recognize what is on the other end in all their/its soul glory;

   Thank that person, place, or thing for the lessons learned from this connection;

7) Visualize a complete severing of the cord with a knife or by burning the cord from yourself to whatever is on the other end;

8) Say the following: "I, (state your name), hereby release and sever all cords to you that do not serve and support our highest good. As I cut the ties to you, I honour myself, and I honour you. We each stand free in our own light. Only that which is beneficial and empowering remains."

Education can replace fear, and new intelligence can create new power, and new courage. If you were afraid of the idea of cords, attachments, or encountering lower energies in your mediumship, allow this new information to take the place of the fear. All energies begin as neutral and over time, become imbued with qualities that we perceive as higher or lower, positive or negative. As form beings, we have so many aspects of power – physical, mental, emotional, and spiritual. And using these powers, we are able to detach, remove, and transmute energies all the time. You are so much more powerful than you may yet believe.

There are times when it is important to set aside your fear and the feeling that you need to protect yourself, and to step instead into your strength, courage, and power. Imagine for a moment that you notice your energy drop after an encounter (either a reading or another interaction). Before you activate your protective armor, take a moment to tune in to the essence of what is really going on. Once you know what that is, you can then respond with intelligence, power, and love instead of with fear, defensiveness, and worry.

Chapter Eight

Go Ahead, Take the Stage!

§

Platform (gallery) or group mediumship, whether on a stage or even just with a private, small group, gives us a chance to demonstrate continuity of the soul to a number of people at once, and this is why it is one of my favourite things to do! You will likely enjoy it too once you become comfortable with it.

As exciting as platform work can be, we want to avoid platforms or groups unless and until we are trained to do it. And that is the intention in this chapter; to prepare you with information, techniques, and strategies to deliver a successful and skillful gallery-style reading.

Platform mediumship is different than private-sitting mediumship. Not in terms of the process of connecting with spirit, but in its technique. And not knowing these differences in technique will make for a poor group experience. Thankfully, you are in the right place to avoid a poor experience and by contrast, create a fantastic event that everyone will enjoy, including you.

It is not uncommon for folks to attend a group or gallery reading and not want to receive a reading. Hearing from spirit can be a very vulnerable experience for someone, especially in a group. Yet, those same people are often curious and interested in witnessing mediumship - without participating - and learning more about how it works. In this way, platform readings allow for those nervous about mediumship to see transformation in others without having to be vulnerable themselves.

Journal Exercise

When thinking about standing on a stage or in front of a group, are there any fears that come up for you? If so, journal what they are. What are some ways you might be able to alleviate these fears? Get creative. For example, if you are fearful or nervous of a group of people staring at your physical body, then plan to do a group practice reading sitting down. That might make you feel more comfortable to begin with. Further in the chapter you may find solutions to some other fears.

One of the most common fears in platform work is the fear of getting things wrong in front of a crowd, and there are a couple of ways to address those fears. Remember that as soon as you begin to register fear, it throws off your focus. In mediumship, your focus needs to be on the other, on the people you read for and help. Shift your focus from your own insecurities back to the people who have come to see you; they are hoping that you will bring something through for them from the other side. Hold on to that focus, because it holds the energy of service, which is also love. And you know in order to blend with spirit most effectively, your consciousness or your vibrational frequency needs to be a very close match to the spirit world. So, stay in the love, not in the fear.

What about those insecurities though? How can you deal with them in a very real way? You need to tend to most of them long before deciding to get on a stage in front of a crowd of people. Most of the fears people have about platform mediumship (being repetitively wrong or no one in your audience recognizing a spirit you are bringing through) can be quelled over time by engaging in as many practice group readings as you can. You will want to learn well in advance of a large, professional platform reading how to handle it when something does not make sense to a sitter (see below) or when no one in your audience recognizes a spirit person (see below), and how to feel at ease during the platform. The key here is to give yourself enough group-reading experiences in a safe environment, such as in classes or by offering free group-readings. These settings alleviate expectations and allow for a low pressure opportunity to experience spirit, yourself, and an audience, all together.

You will want to prepare for a platform in the same way you prepare for private mediumship. Clear your energy, call in your guides, angels, loved ones and spirit helpers, center yourself, and open your energy centres. Expand and raise the vibration of your auric field through breath work and meditation, while working to generate positive energies within your heart. It is best to find a private area in which to prepare where you will not be disturbed. Another element to consider about platform or group mediumship is that working in the presence of a large number of people can amplify the energy of grief. While this is not always true, and groups can also generate wonderful, joyful energy, you will want to make sure your vibrational frequency is not affected by the energy of grief ahead of time. For this reason, be sure not to mingle in the energy ahead of your reading, but rather, wait until afterward to personally meet and greet some of your audience. If you become impacted by the lower energy of grief in the room, your own vibrational frequency will drop, and guess what will happen? Your ability to connect with spirit will be impaired. So, prepare well for your high vibrational state, and take good care to stay in that zone during the entire platform, regardless of the overwhelming energy of grief that may surround you. See it, acknowledge it, understand it is there, and have compassion for it. But do not let it in. If you do, your ability to deliver the gift of mediumship may be compromised.

Just as in private sittings, you must prepare your platform audience so they understand what to expect and how you work with spirit, specifically. Your audience preparation should include sharing some the following information:

1. The Language of Spirit: Explain to your audience how spirit communicates with you. Most people think spirit people just 'talk' to us as mediums, and we relay that information without interpretation. As you know, this is not how it works. The language of spirit is mostly symbolic. When a spirit person blends with you, they transmit information to you in a number of ways through the clair-senses (clairvoy-

ance, clairaudience, clairsentience, claircognizance). You then interpret or translate much of that information before passing it along to the person receiving the reading. And of course, there will also be literal information communicated where you will not have to do any translating. The language of spirit alternates between literal and symbolic, constantly.

2. Lineup of Spirit People: As a single person delivering messages to a number of people, you will not be able to deliver messages from all of the spirit people who show up. You will have a long lineup of people who would like to communicate with you from the other side. It is important your audience is informed that if they do not hear from someone in spirit that day, it does not mean their person in spirit is not there. It is just that you will not be able to bring through all of the present souls in the hour or two you have with them. It is just a timing thing that the audience must understand.

3. Who Might Show Up: Sometimes surprising visits happen. It is important your audience knows that anyone connected to them, directly or indirectly, can show up. An example of a spirit who is connected indirectly could be a co-worker's child who

passed. The spirit person is not related to the person in the audience, but they may have a message they want passed along.

4. What Is Needed from the Audience: This is all about body language and open hearts. Let your audience know that in order to stay open energetically, they cannot cross their arms (sometimes not even their legs). They need to stay open and allow themselves to believe that if something comes through that makes sense for them, they are allowed to claim it. And we need them to. If something makes sense and someone does not claim it, that spirit connection will just fade away because it is not being validated, and another stronger connection will come in.

5. Piggy-Backed Messages: This occurs when multiple spirits come through you at once based on their similarities. For example, you could deliver fifteen points of validation to your gallery and it still makes sense for two separate audience members. When this happens – whether or not you are aware of it – you have two spirits communicating with you at once. The information is illustrating it as such, and it is not uncommon as a medium to be unaware that multiple spirits are communicating at the same time.

Once your gallery is prepared with knowledge about how it all works and what is needed from them, it is time for you to begin. You may wish to lead your audience in a short meditation to open the energy in the space, or you may just straight away go in to your first reading - whichever feels most appropriate for you.

In contrast to a private sitting which lasts anywhere from thirty to sixty minutes typically, platform gives you generally five to ten minutes per reading (may be shorter or longer depending on your personal style or your audience size - think group of several hundred vs. ten or twenty). This means you will not be able to go through all of the standard questions you would typically ask spirit in a private sitting. Rather, a reading from the stage or platform requires a slightly different approach from traditional, private-sitting mediumship.

In a platform, there are a couple of ways to begin a reading:

1. First, you may begin with something very specific and narrow to identify the person in the audience you are reading for. This might be something like a name (of the spirit person or someone in the audience), a very specific way of passing, a very specific item, or a select and important word. Here is one such example; "I have

a younger female coming through and she wants me to say the name, Christine. Who can connect with this?" Another example might be; "I have a father energy stepping forward, and when he comes to me I understand his background is Italian and that he left behind a coin collection. Who can understand this?"

2. Your second option is to begin the traditional way by establishing the gender and the relationship to the sitter and possibly the cause of their passing. Then, within the same sentence, you might note something unique about the spirit person. For instance; "I have an older female stepping forward, and she comes to me with a contemporary energy as a sister or friend. I know from her that her passing is sudden and unexpected and there is some trauma and tragedy around this passing. She says to me that she worked or volunteered in education. Who does this resonate with?"

When you are new to platform or stage work, it is a good idea to have a script of questions for your first couple of readings. Otherwise, you are likely to get lost in the stars for a moment and not remember what to ask! As you know, if you do not take control of the information exchange by asking spirit questions, spirit is likely to download a ton of information onto you without any context or order. When they do that, it is hard to present the information in a clear way to your audience, and you may end up presenting a large volume of information without context or concept. As a result, your audience will have to do more work than you to figure it out. This is a by-product of being nervous. So, make your plan ahead of time by deciding which questions you are going to ask for at least the first one or two readings on the stage.

One of the nice things about being an advanced or professional medium is that you remember all of the questions to ask spirit in a private sitting. You do not need to rely on reading them from a paper anymore. You have done it enough that it becomes nearly automatic for you to cover all of the information you need to ascertain from spirit in a reading. In platform readings however, we really cannot repeat the questions from one reading to another. We must change it up because you have an audience watching each of those readings, and if we do not change up the questions, we will become predictable to the audience. Such predictability can drain the energy of the audience. Included below is a list of questions to ask and information to present in a gallery reading. You will notice a lot of these questions are the same as in private sittings; however, in platform readings, we only get to ask a few of these each time rather than all of them as we do in a private reading.

Questions to Launch Your Gallery Reading

- Male/Female/Other?
- Age: Younger/Older/In between/ Child?
- Physical Appearance (at least one aspect of it, only if possible, but not necessary)?
- What caused their passing?
- Personality?
- Relationship to the sitter?
- Hobbies/Interests/Work?
- What have they seen the sitter doing recently?
- Shared Memory?
- Memento?
- Special Dates?
- Special Names?
- Do they have children? How many? Boy/girl makeup?
- What did their house look like/where did they live?
- Who are they with on the other side?
- Who greeted them at transition or what was the scene around their passing?
- Is there something special about the sitter they'd like to acknowledge?

Often during a platform reading, you can become overwhelmed by the number of spirits trying to blend with you. When this happens, we need to be sure to make a clear and focused decision on which spirit we are choosing to bring through. Hone your focus toward their energy. If you are unsure which spirit to choose, choose the one who is communicating most easily and clearly, even if that unfortunately means you have to disregard a quieter spirit who is struggling to communicate with you. Simply let them know you will do your best to either come back to them, or ask them to up their energy to get a better line of communication.

Energetic ties are a very real phenomenon in mediumship. What this means is that you will want to position yourself so that your entire audience is in front of you – not to your side, or behind you. Keep them in front of you so that you have a direct physical pathway to them and their energy. This may sound like a small point, but it can make all the difference in the world in making the connection clearer between yourself, spirit, and whomever you may be reading for in the audience.

Once you feel you have represented a spirit person well in your platform reading, it is time to move to the message. By now, you may be quite experienced in delivering validating and powerful messages. Nevertheless, there are some changes in protocol when it comes to delivering messages to a group versus in a private sitting. Types of messages that are okay to deliver privately are not necessarily appropriate in front of an audience. An example could be a message about a drug or alcohol addiction taking place in the family of the sitter or for the sitter themselves. It is not acceptable to expose the sitter to this type of vulnerability in front of an audience. Another example could be a deep personal struggle with suicidal thoughts or prior abuse. Again, this type of information is private and inappropriate to disclose in front of a group. If these types of messages come up, be prepared to word them in more generic ways that do not specify the subject matter exactly. Or, you could simply ask spirit for something else. You may also choose to deliver a message about these sorts of things after your gallery - if you can find a way to communicate with the intended recipient privately.

Some potentially challenging situations can arise in a platform reading that have the potential to make you feel nervous, and which may shrink your auric field, thus diminishing its quality. If this occurs, it will also diminish your ability to channel spirit. So it is best to discuss these things now so you can learn how to move through them should they occur, thus keeping your energy in check.

One of the most challenging things that can happen on a platform is no one taking the spirit person you are bringing through. If this occurs, what is likely happening is that a remote connection to someone in the room — a distant relative, say, or perhaps someone who knows them through someone else — is coming through but is not recognized by the audience member. This can also happen in a private reading, but we tend to have more time to explore it as compared to the time we have in a gallery-style reading. It is also possible (believe it or not) that the person the spirit belongs to in the audience is too afraid or nervous to acknowledge them. Other times still, you may have interpreted or presented a piece of information in a way that is just slightly out of sync from what spirit intended, and so what you have presented may not be recognized. Whatever the reason, if you experience this situation, simply tell your audience, "I am going to set this person aside for now and move on to another spirit here with me now." Simple as that, and then you can move on. Just stop thinking about it, and open up to receive another spirit in your energy.

Another potentially difficult situation on a platform is when an audience member who, although acknowledging the information coming through as making sense to them, still has an attitude or tone that is harsh or skeptical.

Responding to this by trying to soften their energy can waste a lot of time. The best way to handle this is to deliver the information quickly and move on. The sooner you are done working with them, the better preserved your own energy will be.

Platform mediumship, over time, will reveal parts of yourself to yourself. You will find your own unique style with which you feel comfortable, and you will learn how best to engage your audience, which, by the way, should usually include some lightheartedness and humour. The power of laughter is huge in a room full of grief, so never underestimate the need for a few jokes!

When approaching group or platform work, it is often best to scale it up, from less intimidating to more intimidating. Think about scheduling a practice group reading of three to five people, and after you are comfortable with that size audience, move up to a group of ten, and so on. If it becomes something you really enjoy, move on to an event, perhaps on an actual stage with a large audience. I highly recommend practicing group readings a number of times before adding this service to your professional offerings. Some mediums find the change in technique a challenge, so be sure to allow yourself the time and experience required to get comfortable with the differences from private to public mediumship demonstrations. Finally, you do not need to practice platform mediumship if you feel it is not for you, or at least, not for you right now. There are many professional mediums who spend most of their time in private sittings, and not with groups. Honour what feels right for you, always.

Chapter Nine

Power in the Message

§

In mediumship, many of the people who come to see you will be in some state of grieving. It is important to be able to observe them in order to understand where they are operating from at the time you see them. Are they excited just to experience mediumship, or are they distraught with grief? Do they feel devastated, or in a state of high vibration and would just like to talk to their spirit family? Meeting people where they are is an important part of advanced mediumship. You will need to assess where someone is, energetically, very quickly so that you can determine how to approach them. For example, if a client is in the midst of feeling deep loss, is it best to open with something light and humorous or would it be better to open with a compassionate, soft greeting? Conversely, if a client is very open and simply excited to have an experience with spirit, is it best to open with soft, comforting, emotional language and offer them a tissue, or is it best to match their tempo with an excited energy that makes them feel welcome? We want to meet clients where they are, emotionally and mentally. Now, this does not mean we match them, vibrationally; it simply means we allow them to feel seen and important, and we do that by entering their energy in a way that makes them feel safe and understood. We let them know we see them by meeting them with the kind of energy that is in tune with them.

This is where your empathic abilities (the ability to feel someone else's emotions) need to be supported by establishing good boundaries. As mediums, we want to compassionately observe where the client is at, but we do not want to feel their emotions as our own. If you do that, and as we have previously discussed, you will drop your own frequency to the point that you likely will not blend successfully with spirit.

In an advanced mediumship practice, the power and relevance of the messages you deliver are all-important. Basic messaging of "they love you and they are with you" is, of course, insufficient. Your messages must be accurate, useful, and pertinent to the sitter's life. This does not mean we should not communicate that spirit loves them and that they visit often, but this alone is not enough.

As an advanced medium you also want to be skilled enough to take questions from your client – questions they would like to ask their loved ones. Sometimes, it is these questions that constitute the message portion of the reading. Other times, you will do both – take questions from your client as well as deliver messages to the client from spirit. It is up to you to feel out which or both ways of proceeding will fulfill the sitters' needs.

But not all questions are appropriate. Understand and explain to your client that spirit communication is not direct and linear, and as a medium, you also have to be able to interpret a spirit's answer when it is not communicated literally. Remind them that the language of spirit is most often symbolic and that we do not have traditional 'conversations' with spirit people. Certain types of questions should be avoided or if necessary, rejected. These are what I call "trick pony' questions, such as, "Ask her what my middle name is." Again, demonstration of the continuity of life beyond form is made through the body of evidence presented throughout a reading, not through a single point of validation. Appropriate questions can be many things. For example: "She wanted me to take her ashes to the sea – is she happy I did that?" Or, "My sister and I have gone through some hard times since his passing – can you ask him what I should do?" I always instruct students to include some level of validation in the answer as well, especially if it is a yes/no answer.

Powerful messages in a mediumship reading contain a two-fold approach. We need to validate that the premise of the message is correct before we deliver the message. For example, we cannot say, "Spirit says your relationship with your child is disconnected and that to reconnect with them, consider taking time away from devices and spend more quality time together", unless of course we have validated that it is in fact true that their relationship with their child is strained. Instead, you want to present the information in two stages. First, we might say "Spirit makes me feel your relationship with your child is feeling particularly strained right now - is that true?" From there, if this information is validated, you would move on to the message about spending more quality time together without devices. Approaching the message in this two-tiered way, gives you a chance to clarify with spirit that the basis of the message is correct before presenting what really needs to be expressed through the end-of-reading message.

In addition to the two-fold approach for messaging, we also want to be sure to present a message of relevance and pertinence to the sitter's life, as well as being validating. You may ask spirit about an important issue that came up during the reading and see if they have a message to help support their loved ones here or, you may simply open the floor to spirit. Say, "what would you like to say to your person here?" Remember that readings can be for the growth and healing of both the client and the spirit person. We often think those left behind are the only ones needing a mediumship reading, but there have been many occasions when, in the process of relaying a message to someone here in the physical world, the spirit person transmitting the message was finally able to carry forward with their own soul's journey. So, if a message seems to be simplified, basic and inconsequential to your client, or even if it seems obscure and complicated, relay the message every single time. Its importance or relevance may be far beyond your initial sense.

Chapter Ten

Spirit in the Age of Technology

§

Mediums have come a long way from giving readings in secret rooms with dark curtains drawn. The most common types of mediumship have changed too. One hundred years ago, seeing a medium would most commonly entail visiting someone who would attempt to demonstrate continuity of the soul through physical means – through physical mediumship. These demonstrations might have included transfiguration, rappings, table tipping, automatic writing, trances, and the like.

Over time, mediumship practice has largely moved away from physical demonstrations, and spirit communication has evolved more on mental terms, through the development and practice of mental mediumship. Mental mediumship involves the medium receiving and interpreting information from spirit through the mind. Why has this shift occurred; why did we move away from physical mediumship? Physical demonstrations, certainly in the late 19th and early 20th centuries, were easily faked. Personal ambitions of individuals looking for fame and notoriety were commonplace in new spiritual communities, and unfortunately, this led to hoaxes and fraudulent demonstrations of mediumship. The multitude of debunked claims of physical mediumship is what, I believe, really laid the pathway for the persecution and suspicion of all mediums over the course of centuries even to today. Of course, this does not mean there are not or were not legitimate physical mediums. But I believe there were more fake ones than real ones, and because of this, it makes sense that real spirit communicators shifted away from physical demonstrations.

I have always practiced and been connected to mental mediumship with the exception of automatic writing, which I enjoy doing every so often. My formal educational background is in science; environmental technology to be exact.

I am very naturally a left-brained thinker. Evidence is important to me. Proof is important to me. Mental mediumship, from my view and experience, is a much more reliable and fraud-proof way of proving the existence of life-after-life as compared to physical mediumship. Good mental mediumship consists of providing a volume of information that is verifiable and accurate. Good mediumship does not consist of one or two pieces of good, correct information, but rather a body of work, or a body of evidence that substantially illustrates a spirit person. As the demonstration of spirit presence has evolved, so too has the way we connect spirit to their loved ones here in the physical world. It has changed hugely. Three years into a global pandemic in 2023, the way we communicate with each other, human-to-human, has changed equally as much. Over the past three years, because of the pandemic, effectively all of the private readings, all gallery readings, all of my speaking and teaching engagements, have been virtual. That is a stark change from ten years ago, when ninety percent of my readings took place in person. And the ten percent that did take place virtually were mostly over the telephone and rarely by video chat as is common today.

People often ask, "Does it still work in the same way? Can you connect with spirit for me, even though we are not sitting in the same room together?" It is fascinating to many clients that the process is exactly the same, and that as mediums, we do not need to be face-to-face with them. The truth is, we are not bound by time and space in spirit communication, so physical boundaries or separations are totally irrelevant to the process.

Prior to the pandemic, many of the mediums training with me were reluctant or nervous about giving virtual readings, whether over video chat, telephone, or email. The best way to alleviate some of those fears was to have them experience the reality first hand – that spirit is not bound by space or time, and that we can have deep connections with them whether or not their living loved one happens to be in the same room as we are.

It is important to know that the three-way dynamic (medium, spirit, sitter) remains the same whether you are reading for someone virtually or in-person. You must contribute to the connection, spirit must, and your sitter must. Your sitter's contribution is essentially staying open – emotionally, mentally, and physically – and using their voice to respond to you. Spirit's contribution is simply a willingness to connect, and the medium's contribution is to be prepared with an open and loving heart.

Virtual readings have made it even more important to check in with your client frequently because a small gesture or acknowledgment can easily be missed in a virtual setting. Checking in is simply asking your client if what you are saying is clear and if the message is making sense. You can use a variety of phrases after each point of validation to confirm accuracy. Checking in might sound like:

> Is this correct?
> Is this true?
> Do you understand this?
> Can you resonate?

Not checking in with a client can become a bad habit, quickly. If we are not checking in, then we are likely railroading our client. Railroading is presenting numerous pieces of information all at once, and not checking that each point is understood and accurate. An example of railroading might be, "Your sister has blonde hair and says to me she passed suddenly and the month of May is important, and she also tells me that she has a daughter she left behind who misses her very much – can you understand this?" In this statement, four pieces of validation have been provided, but the sitter has only been asked at the end of the four points if it makes sense to them. What if only two of the four points make sense? Then what? How is your client supposed to answer you? The better way to present this information might sound like this: "Your sister comes to me with light or blonde hair – is this correct? I also understand from her that she made her departure from the physical world suddenly and unexpectedly, do you understand this? She brings up the month of May as significant for her – can you place this? She also wants to acknowledge a daughter here in the physical world, is this true, does she have a daughter?" By checking in, you are creating an opportunity to not only understand and gauge your accuracy as your reading progresses, but you are also creating the opportunity to explore context or gain more clarity from spirit when something does not make sense the way you have presented it.

Despite the fact that we have changed, our communication methods have changed, and attitudes about spirit and mediumship have changed (in a positive direction), the nature of spirit remains the same as it has ever been - it is pure love. How we communicate with them as mental mediums is also the same – nothing has changed over the past years. So rest assured that no matter how you are called to connect spirit to their people here in the physical world, your internal process and spirit's responsiveness to good and solid preparation will be exactly the same. Repeat after me: Whenever I show up, spirit shows up.

Chapter Eleven

Taking Care of Yourself

§

Playing small refers to the part in each of us that is focused on short-term, temporary comfort, security and validation. Playing small usually means we dismiss what we really want in life in order to maintain an illusion of security or control. Conversely, playing big means we are willing to experience short-term discomfort or uncertainty in the service of what we truly want, like experiencing greater love and connection with others, living with purpose, and living with freedom of self. Playing small means our actions are motivated by our fears and insecurities, and playing big means our actions are motivated by what brings us true fulfillment. In playing big, our actions and decisions necessitate that we summon up courage, faith, and trust. Whether we play small or big has nothing to do with the size of our goals or our accomplishments. It is more about the underlying beliefs we have about ourselves and about life that drive how we approach our own lives - big or small.

As your mediumship journey continues to unfold and unravel and grow and change, consider committing to being open to the reality that your vision of how you want to live your life will evolve, and that is okay. Consider committing to having the types of experiences you want to have in your life – like connections, being loved, feeling freedom, feeling peace, learning, etc. Let your vision or plan be in service to these things, and be sure to take time for you. If you talk to anyone in the metaphysical community who has worked in the field of mediumship or energy healing for any appreciable number of years, you will hear stories of burnout and physical illness and general fatigue. Spending so much time in the company of people who are struggling in life without taking the time to rest and to replenish, clear, and rejuvenate yourself can have lasting effects. This is not intended to deter you from becoming a professional medium but rather, it is meant to stress the importance of taking care of yourself, first and foremost.

Running on empty can be commonplace when starting anything new – whether a new business or a new practice or hobby. And while one can usually sustain going all in for some time, it never works in the long-term. Running on empty for the long-term can sometimes result from a sense of scarcity – the notion that you cannot take a break. Change that belief! We are only as good in caring for others as we are in caring for ourselves. Self-care, as a lightworker, has got to be your top priority, or burnout is a very real possibility.

Such exhaustion – or heavy cording from connections you have made in your work – may take years to develop, but it will show up at some point. When it does, take it as a message from the universe to take better care of yourself. Listen to your body. Rest. Eat well. Take time for yourself. Clear your energy often – daily when you are working with the spirit world and other people's energy. And really live life. Love more. Laugh more. Do less. Get the message? Good!

Some of my self-care regimen to keep my personal energy high, clear, and well-rested includes:

1. Daily salt baths;
2. Restful sleep;
3. Listening to what my body is asking

for (this was one that took me a lot of burning out to learn. It was easy for me to listen to my soul's needs and respond accordingly, but my physical body was never a priority for me until it crashed a few times! It was through that suffering that I learned the true value of physical health and wellness);

4. Quiet time;
5. Intentionally leaving blank space in the calendar;
6. Acupuncture;
7. Massage;
8. Soothing oils and creams;
9. Time in nature and with animals;
10. Practicing and expressing gratitude and appreciation;
11. Limiting my time in low-vibration conversations;
12. Expressing love, understanding, kindness, and compassion;
13. Living without expectations of other people;
14. Living without expectations of myself;
15. Clearing my personal energy field daily.

As public mediums, there is a fine line to be distinguished between being courageous/playing big, and being overly ambitious. I think that can be true in any vocation. I remember years ago, my philosophy toward opportunity in my mediumship was that I would say yes to everything. As a young person trying to make a successful life, I think most people adopt a similar philosophy, and I do not think it is a terrible thing for short periods. But prolonged periods will often lead to burnout – the expenditure of energy beyond what you have to give to stay healthy and balanced. It took me a long time to figure out that I do not need to say yes to everything. In fact, I do not need to say yes to anything! Rather than responding immediately to opportunities, I learned that it works best for me to pause, sit with it, and then determine if I want to participate. This pause allows me to really evaluate, both in the mind and in the heart, if something is right for me, and sometimes more importantly, if the timing is right for me.

We often believe we are responsible for the happiness of others. If we are good people and do the right thing, the universe will in turn take care of our happiness. This is a powerless, victim mentality. Learn to identify this and take personal responsibility for what you truly want. You are your own authority.

The confidence-lacking parts of us believe something must be wrong if we are facing a challenge. But when we shift into our higher mind, we understand that what we truly want in life is on the other side of these temporary discomforts. Learn to see that challenges are opportunities for growth. You can be very deliberate in thinking most often about what you want rather than what you do not want. We become what we think, and the essence of what we become is what we attract toward us. Keeping your thoughts in good order is ever important in living an empowered, inspired life.

After a number of successes in life and in particular your mediumship, you will eventually realize the fulfillment you were looking for is not on the other side of a finish line. Delivering a powerful reading where you got the name of the spirit person, teaching a course, giving a public mediumship demonstration – these are all terrific accomplishments. But there is no goal in the world that once achieved will give you complete and total satisfaction. As humans, we tend to experience fulfillment through continued growth and continued experiences, perpetually throughout a lifetime. It will be helpful to keep this in mind and learn to get past your small self's need for validation. Instead, focus on service rather than performance. Once you are in the role of professional medium and you have taken up the sacred agreement with spirit to be their messenger, it is not about you any longer. It is about what makes a difference and helps others. This is the essence of genuine spiritual service, and when you align your motivations with this essence, the universe will open up for you and your practice in marvelous ways.

Chapter Twelve

Manifesting and Living a Spirit-Connected Life

§

Years of readings, psychic investigations, energy clearings, and spirit contact have created mounds of stories in my life that are sometimes described as "out of this world". My husband, Ryan, often says, "You just can't make this stuff up - something always happens around you!", and, "If I weren't living this life with you, I'd never believe that these things really do happen."

You see, being in tune with the subtle energies around and within you, and indeed within the universe at large, makes for an ongoing live-feed of awareness between not only what (and who) is around you, but also what is coming toward you in time. I am a big manifestor. I have found it very genuinely uncomplicated to *become* the energy of the experience or role I would like to have well before the outer experience enters my world. This is the key to manifesting - becoming, in essential form, or, becoming the energy of that which you would like to be or experience *before* the achievement takes place. But I am also aware that part of manifesting with ease comes from being aware of appropriate timing and being aware of one's own soul plan, even in a fleeting way - enough to discern if something is an appropriate pathway for you and if the timing is right. There are currents of energy that usher possibilities into experience, and being aware of those currents, what they will support and what they will not, can help lead you away from dead ends and closed doors, and set you on a better pathway.

Often it is as easy as asking the internal question - is this the right pathway for me, right now? For me, I tend to have an innate draw toward something that I am meant to explore. A spark of inspiration emerges from within me, and away I go with brainstorming and creating. But I have done this long enough to know that, although I am inspired and feel very compelled to create or become or experience something new, the optimal timing may not be in the now. Sometimes the creation period is appropriate in the now, but the share or the launch period is some time in the future. I trust however, when the inspiration comes, I am to act on it and begin working toward it, as should you.

The creation of my television show, Ghosts of Dufferin County and Beyond, is a key example of what can happen when we listen to our internal inspiration, tune into the energy around us, and become aware of the currents of energy that are running through the space and time you are occupying. I remember driving across town one day, and began thinking of visiting haunted locations and investigating them to determine what really is going on. That seemingly random thought was actually a spark of spirit-guided inspiration entering my awareness. I recognized it as such because in a very short period (a matter of minutes) I could visualize the entire idea coming to fruition. I had investigated many homes and businesses for clients who had reported concerns and discomforts from otherworldly experiences, and they needed help to sort it out. And while I enjoyed this work very much, I felt tremendously called to share the message in a bigger way that really, we have nothing to be afraid of when it comes to these occurrences. As form bodies, we inherently have more substantial power than anything in non-form, and we do not need to be afraid or displaced by energies from the spirit world or beyond. How could I achieve this? The inspiration and idea that came to me was that I could achieve this by sharing my work of psychic investigation and energy clearing on a larger scale - on a tv show!

I began putting ideas together and submitting pitches to production companies. After a number of meetings where producers had differing ideas of what would be interesting to an audience, from missing persons cases, to psychic talent shows, none of them clicked and felt right to me, and none of them had the same essence as my initial inspiration. Just a short while later, I connected with a local-to-me television producer through an acquaintance, and met with him to present my pitch. Boom. He immediately loved it, and it was a perfect fit for what he had been looking for. How often is a producer looking for a psychic-medium television show? The timing was perfect, and very spirit-led, obviously! It was brilliant fun to explore such fascinating locations and characters in the three seasons we filmed.

I can remember another day when I was 'daydreaming'. But really I was just tuning in - being receptive - to spirit and my higher self. I envisioned myself and a number of other leading psychic-mediums (no one in particular was clear at the time) hosting an online summit where we would teach and demonstrate the best-of-the-best in mediumship. Within a month, that quick and fleeting inspiration became the Canadian Mediumship Summit hosted by myself and a number of other top-rated Canadian psychic mediums. And two months after that, it was a sold out, incredibly powerful event that saw student mediums from across North America learning and expanding their own talents.

The manifestation of anything, is real. When something is possible for us, and we can get into alignment with its energy, it will enter in to our experience.

Even writing this book, or my first one, or the many articles I have written for various publications, or media interviews or consultations - all of these wonderful experiences I have had as a medium began with small sparks of inspiration, which I know were moments of spirit guiding me. So, notice the small thoughts that animate you enough that you can see and feel a reality that is yet to arrive. Follow the draw, no matter how outrageous or unlikely, because if you became aware of it, there is a reason for that...and the reason is that it is a pathway with your name on it, either right now or in the future. Do not be afraid to shed old skin and step into new endeavours, because in the long run of a life, you are more likely to regret the things you did not dare to do than the things you did.

I could never name and describe all of the synchronistic events that have occurred in my life, nor could I enumerate all the times spirit has nudged me from the other side, whether through feathers landing in my pathway, seeing cardinals or hummingbirds, or dimes falling from the clear blue sky to tell me I was on the right track. But I can tell you that if your life has not already begun to be intertwined with the spirit world, in both helpful and mysterious ways, it is coming - it will happen. And it will be wonderful.

Another way that I receive communication from spirit, angels, guides, my higher self, and the universe at large, is through repetitive number sequences. It is part of the way I live my life to notice them when they appear, and to act on them accordingly. I highly recommend that you pay attention to these most obvious signals, especially if you are still developing your abilities to be in tune with all the energies around you. While there are many resources with repetitive number meanings, below is a quick guide for you to reference when repetitive numbers begin showing up if they have not already!

Repeating 0s: Listen to yourself and your own intuition. Look for signs from the universe and respond accordingly without delay. Keep your thoughts in good order, as you are manifesting out in front of yourself. You are a powerful force, part of the greater whole of the universe, forever connected. Believe in your own power.

Repeating 1s: Pay attention to persistent and repetitive thoughts you are having, because they are a pathway into a direction you are encouraged to travel. When the numbers present, ask yourself at that very moment, what was I just thinking about? Was it positive, or was it negative? Manage your thoughts positively, as you will create in your life whatever it is that you persistently think about, and you are heading into significant manifesting mode. So, think more about what you do want than what you do *not* want. Opportunities are coming, keep your thoughts aligned with what you want to experience.

Repeating 2s: Stay in harmony in all aspects of your life. Do not engage in conflict, but rather honour yourself and your beliefs and current positions. Everything will work out for your highest good. Stay away from negative interactions. Trust that the best outcomes are being worked out in the background. Seeds you have planted from this balanced and harmonious state are coming into fruition.

Repeating 3s: Anything is possible. New changes you have been thinking about or that have been presented to you are part of your higher calling in this life, so you can step into these changes with faith and trust. The spirits of light are all around you, supporting your mission and goals. Stay connected with them and ask for guidance when needed.

Repeating 4s: Angels abound. They are loving and supporting you in every way. Others also tend to come to you for love and support, so give yourself permission to allow the angels to inspire and guide you in your own life, and to help you guide others as well. There is nothing to be afraid of, all will be well. Ask the angels for help and guidance as needed.

Repeating 5s: It is time to turn a new page, to let old doors that are no longer serving you close, and step through new openings. It is time to step into purpose in a different way. Transformation is coming, and it is time for you to start living your best life as you see fit.

Repeating 6s: Keep your thoughts focused on what you want. They may currently be out of order or out of balance. Tend to your own wounds and needs, and give love and help to others with generosity. Ask for help where needed at this time, and be receptive to receiving it. Stay focused on your spiritual self, as this will help you through the process and to gain better control over your thoughts.

Repeating 7s: You are on the right path. All of your hard work is creating fruitful rewards, so keep on this track. You are being commended from spirit for your good work.
Repeating 8s: Pay attention to finances. Make good decisions in this regard, because although you are always supported from the spirit world, you must make sound decisions in your own life. Stay in the flow of good decision-making and there will be positive rewards to come, along with financial prosperity in the future.

Repeating 9s: You are a pillar of light to others. Keep sharing your light. The world needs you and your talents, and you are encouraged to live your purpose by teaching and showing others how to step deeper in to their own power.

As wonderful as it can be to tune in to nonform energies and receive clear signs from the universe all the time, there can sometimes be collateral damage when working as a medium. For me, the collateral damage, if I can call it that, is the storing of memories in my mind that do not actually belong to me. Working as a medium brings along with it many people's experiences of physical death. Sometimes the manner in which someone departs the physical world is traumatic, and as mediums, we hear the stories of what happened - from spirit or from our clients. We learn of all kinds of deaths, and many of the really tough ones never really leave our psyche, entirely. I remember a lot of firsts in my history of readings. I remember the first spirit who came to me who had been murdered. As a soul, he was fine. He had transitioned, but the story he told me about his departure was heavy. It was hard to relive and relay as a point of validation, but I did it. I remember reading for a client whose grandchild had sleep-walked into a lake and drowned. They never found him until the morning. I remember a client whose son had fallen in a well, and another whose child had been crushed by a pile of wood, and yet another whose child had been struck by a car while walking down the street. You see, as mediums, we store these memories that have nothing to do with things we may have actually experienced in our own lives. It is because of this that we must always take good care of our own energies, and our own mental health. We must purge our energy fields and minds of the memories that do not originate with us in order to stay in a high vibration and not be haunted by all the stories we have heard, literally every working day of our lives.

Each of us takes care of our mental, emotional, and energetic states in different ways. For me, when I have a reading with particularly traumatic elements, I have always found it helpful to talk about it afterward. Without revealing any identifiable information, I share with my husband. I talk through it. Over the years he has developed the ability to listen to me without becoming disturbed or overwhelmed. He hears me, acknowledges what I have said, offers a small amount of personal insight, and then we move on from it. This brief discussion is a useful practice for me to release the memory from occupying much space in my mind. Other times, I require a full and total energy clearing to release the seeds of memory that implanted in my mind. Find what works for you, and practice it often.

Chapter Thirteen

Parting Words
Hold Your Power while Sharing your Light

§

It is a courageous act to go out into this world as a medium. Why does it take courage to do this work? To answer this question, we must consider and examine history.

The vocations of medium, psychic, intuitive, empath, and witch all have a long history. Perhaps they are among the longest-standing occupations. There are very old stories from around the world about the persecuted, the misunderstood, the executed, the castaways, the weird ones. As living beings who practice these callings now, we remember those stories, deep in our very bones. We remember the people, too, whether they are our ancestors or characters in the world's history, not just our own family's. We remember the stories and the people most significantly by seeing ourselves in them; when we identify with them; when we realize that indeed we are them, but existing in the present. We are the witches, the seers, the strange ones. We are all the names that history has ever given us. But, as empowered humans, let us now choose what we are to be called and how we are to be described. If we choose to use the same names from history, let us do so because we choose to, and let us reclaim the power of those words for our own definition and use. Or, let us choose new words that reflect who we are now, with power, love, and intelligence.

It is natural to remember the experiences of those who came before us, and it is natural to wonder about the harsh judgment we might endure when the world sees us. But these are the kinds of fears that keep us small. They keep our lights dim, and sometimes, even prevent us from truly living on purpose. A soul's purpose never abandons the life in which it resides, but it is also true that we have free will choice to pick up the cause or not, however heavy; however light.

It is a beautiful demonstration of the power of an enduring spirit to see that even with everything our predecessors suffered, under centuries and lifetimes of oppression and ostracization, we have survived. We are still here helping others heal and expand their own consciousness. And why is that? Why did we survive to still be here doing this sacred work? Because we are needed. Our work and what we do is necessary in this world now and in the past. We are the helpers – the bringers of the light, and while suffering is part of the human experience, so too will we be needed to serve the souls (ourselves included) through that suffering.

Now it is your time to find the courage to be seen. Close your eyes in this moment, and allow yourself to feel that deep calling in your heart that is steering you. Despite the waves of possible uncertainty or fear, you know this is for you. You know everything that has occurred up to this point has been guiding you to this moment of choosing to show up in this world with power and deep love to offer.

Introducing your authentic, genuine, self as a medium to a world that may or may not be an ally to you can be scary. It can feel vulnerable, even terrifying. You are not alone. Most mediums experience some fear before sharing their gifts with the world. And so I want to prepare you mentally, and logistically, for your new launch into the light.

You might have discovered either in this book or throughout your life that your true and authentic identity originates with you. You do not need to nor should you accept an identity assigned to you by anyone else, and no one can take your power from you. In your spiritual journey, you might have already learned that expressing purpose from the soul sometimes causes people to fall out of your life when your belief systems are very different from each other's. No doubt, you have experienced the wonder of new and marvelous people being drawn into your life. As much as you might have already experienced this, there is more to come as you publicly share and declare your purpose and mission.

As our consciousness changes, we begin to shift into new versions of ourselves and see things through new eyes. Those with whom we previously connected, may no longer fit comfortably in our lives. Our consciousness may become vastly different from one another, and when that happens, they essentially vibrate out of our lives. The immediate reaction when this occurs tends to be trying to mend fences or salvage the relationship or keep things the same. I can tell you for certain that if you go this route – trying to maintain relationships with people who do not accept you as a medium – you will no doubt betray yourself. Your power will dissipate. Tap into that deep space of love for yourself, in your own heart, that says to you, "I am the only person I need approval from. No one's approval is needed by me. I love me, and that is enough." We must allow ourselves to be who we are. We must love and accept ourselves in a way that reflects our free choice, and honour our own and others' freedom to do what feels right and appropriate for each one of us.

Life is always a series of opening and closing doors, and one of the biggest life challenges anyone can have is to find peace with the discomfort of changing relationships. Trying to fix a relationship by altering who we are and what we inherently deserve, does not help anyone. Rather, if we allow it to be what it is, and refrain from requiring ourselves or the other to abandon what feels right and good just for the sake of achieving harmony, we will find comfort in surrendering to the situation and allowing the experience to show us something. Because the harmony will not be real anyway. There will be an underlying tension - a sense of not being true-to-self that will prevail. As a result, tensions will eventually arise and conflict will occur anyway, because conflict is what surfaces when we outgrow a relationship.

You will be challenged by the beliefs of others that are not aligned with yours. It will happen. And early in a professional or advanced practice, you might feel the need to defend or explain yourself to the doubtful minds around you. But you must understand that it is not and never will be our jobs as mediums, to prove anything to anyone. If you do choose to speak to someone about what you do, or give your services to them, you must do so from a place of clarity and certainty. As mediums, our job is to preserve the clarity of our work. It is not our job to convince someone to believe in the afterlife. The certainty aspect relates to knowing we have a choice who we speak to and who we serve. Simply because someone would like to engage us does not mean we have any obligation to connect with them. And so the certainty lies within the knowledge that you have chosen to connect with this person because it feels right and appropriate to do so and not because it may feel right and appropriate only to them.

This also means we get to choose what we share and with whom we share it. And we are under no obligation to reveal ourselves to anyone we feel may threaten our own sense of security and confidence by challenging us to prove something to them. Engaging in debates should be avoided, as you will no doubt get significantly bumped out of your power in the process.

The stories of our lives are sacred parts of us. Indeed, our stories can be so holy that some of us are innately discerning about who we share them with. For others, sharing on a whim feels right and good. Either way is okay as we each respond differently to revealing who we are.

There is so much power wrapped up in the words used to describe who we are based on what we have been through. Our stories are doorways into our own vulnerability; and most certainly, we do not need to invite just anyone into the tender, sometimes-painful, raw and exposed underbelly of who we are or who we were or what we have been through. Sharing our stories is tantamount to bestowing a great honour upon the listener. So why should we not be discerning about who we share with? Compassionate and understanding ears are what the heart searches for here. So let us honour that more often.

This world needs you. You have blazed many trails, and there are so many who have yet to emerge who will need the paths you have made as much as you needed the paths that were made by your predecessors. The wisdom you have gained through exploration and discovery is invaluable. Share that wisdom. Everything you have been through has made you who you are – every bit of consciousness you have activated changes all of us, as it is most certainly true that we are all connected. Your role now is to continue to bring light to the darkest places of human experiences. May we all band together in community, and collectively embrace the truest nature of spirit while in form - which is love.

Whether you came to mediumship out of loss, out of interest, or out of your soul's yearning, it is important to stay in touch with your heart – let your heart lead in your sessions. You may be sitting with your third client of the day, your thirtieth client of the month, and for you, communicating with the dearly departed has become a part of your ordinary, extraordinary reality. But even still, never forget that most of the people coming to sit with you have incredible stories of hardship and of loss, and they need to be seen and known by you, with your compassionate heart. Make every reading count.

Printed in the USA
CPSIA information can be obtained
at www.ICGtesting.com
LVHW081629290124
770261LV00039B/881